BAHIAN RECÔNCAVO PLANTATIONS

BAHIAN RECÔNCAVO PLANTATIONS

Spaces of Power and Resistance

Doriane Andrade Meyer

INSTITUTE FOR THE STUDY OF THE AMERICAS AT THE UNIVERSITY OF NORTH CAROLINA AT CHAPEL HILL

INSTITUTE FOR THE **STUDY** OF THE **AMERICAS**

This book was generously supported by funding from the Office
of the Dean of the College of Arts and Sciences at the University
of North Carolina at Chapel Hill.

Suggested citation: Meyer, Doriane Andrade. *Bahian Recôncavo Plantations:
Spaces of Power and Resistance*. Chapel Hill: Institute for the Study of the
Americas at the University of North Carolina at Chapel Hill, 2023.

DOI: https://doi.org/10.5149/9781469677224_Meyer

Library of Congress Cataloging-in-Publication Data
Names: Meyer, Doriane Andrade, author.
Title: Bahian Recôncavo plantations : spaces of power and
  resistance / Doriane Andrade Meyer.
Other titles: Spaces of power and resistance | Studies in Latin America.
Description: Chapel Hill : Institute for the Study of the Americas at the
  University of North Carolina at Chapel Hill, [2023] | Series: Studies in
  Latin America | Includes bibliographical references.
Identifiers: LCCN 2023020750 | ISBN 9781469677217 (paperback) |
  ISBN 9781469677224 (open access ebook)
Subjects: LCSH: Sugar plantations—Social aspects—Brazil—Recôncavo
  Basin—History. | Enslaved persons—Brazil—Recôncavo Basin—Social
  conditions. | Slavery—Social aspects—Brazil—Recôncavo Basin. |
  Black people—Brazil—Recôncavo Basin—Social conditions. |
  Recôncavo Basin (Brazil)—Race relations—History.
Classification: LCC HD9114.B73 R43 2023 |
  DDC 338.1/736109813—dc23/eng/20230616
LC record available at https://lccn.loc.gov/2023020750

Published by the Institute for the Study of the Americas
at the University of North Carolina at Chapel Hill

Distributed by the University of North Carolina Press
www.uncpress.org

To Leo, my motivation.

For my parents, my inspiration.

Table of Contents

Abstract

Brazil was the recipient of the highest number of enslaved Africans and maintained the longest-lasting system of slavery in the Americas. Over three centuries, approximately four million Africans were brought to Brazil via the Middle Passage. Slavery had a significant impact on most aspects of Brazilian society, but the plantations were particularly emblematic of the spatial systems of exploitation associated with slavery. However, despite being designed to exert control over enslaved Africans, those plantations also served as sites of resistance, where enslaved people found ways to confront the system. Using more than seventy photographs, paintings, and maps, this book focuses on three plantations in the Bahian Recôncavo region and examines how their architecture and geography were used for both control and resistance. It also shows how the legacy of slavery is still evident throughout Brazil today. The existence of more than 100 million Afro-descendant Brazilians living in informal settlements is a reflection of the ongoing social and racial barriers that have persisted since the time of slavery.

KEYWORDS *plantation slavery; African Diaspora; Brazilian architecture; social inequalities; segregation*

Acknowledgments

As a Brazilian from a family with a diverse mix of ancestry from Germany, Italy, Africa, and Portugal, like many others in the country, I have always been fascinated by my family's history and the tales passed down by my parents about our ancestries. Therefore, I begin by thanking my earliest ancestors who arrived in Brazil and acknowledging their strength in building a new life in a land that was vastly different from their own. I particularly honor my African ancestors, who were brought to Brazil through the transatlantic slave trade and did not have a choice in their journey. Their resilience serves as an inspiration to me.

I am very grateful to the ones who first read this research during my PhD at the University of Kansas. My sincerest thanks go to Mahbub Rashid, for his unwavering advising and encouragement throughout my academic journey. He provided invaluable guidance and support during the ups and downs and has been instrumental in my career growth. I would like to express my deep gratitude to Robert Schwaller, who engaged in numerous book discussions with me and expanded my comprehension of slavery in the Americas. His guidance during the revision process of this book was also instrumental in its completion. I want to acknowledge the mentorship of Farhan Karim whose guidance and encouragement woke up my passion for history of architecture. I am also thankful to Jessica Gerschultz and Marie-Alice L'Heureux for the insightful comments and support for my work. At the University of Kansas, I am also grateful for the friendship and encouragement of Luciano Tosta, who first instilled in me the confidence to pursue an academic career and has offered me support throughout. I would also like to express my thanks to Nilou Vakil, Joe Colistra, and Thom Allen for their support during and after my time at the University of Kansas.

These individuals have each played a significant role in my academic journey, and I am deeply grateful for their support through advising, conversations, and recommendations. Other scholars deserve many thanks. They are Marta Caminero-Santangelo, Brent Metz, Cecile Accille, Araceli Masterson-Algar, Kapila Silva, Paola Sanguinetti, Bob Coffeen, and everybody who helped me in any way during my time at KU.

This book was prepared for publication while I held a postdoctorate position at the Yale Gilder Lehrman Center. I am deeply grateful to Michelle Zacks, David Blight, Luis DeBaca, and Phillip Bernstein for their support of my work. Additionally, during my time at Yale, I am grateful for the friendship of João José Reis and Junia Furtado. In the middle of symposiums, lectures, meals, and World Cup games, we had wonderful, enlightening conversations. I would also like to express my appreciation to Cécile Fromont and Stuart Schwartz for their willingness to discuss my work and for being readily available when needed.

I am indebted to the organizations that funded my research and conference trips. Without their support, this work would not have been possible: KU School of Architecture & Design; KU Center for Latin American and Caribbean Studies; KU Graduate Studies; KU Hall Center for the Humanities; KU International Affairs; the Oppenheimer Memorial; the Gill Family Foundation; the Schomburg Center for the Research in Black Culture Center; the Lapidus Center for the Historical Analysis of Transatlantic Slavery; the New York Public Library; the Tinker Foundation; the Yale School of Architecture; the Yale Gilder Lehrman Center; and the Yale MacMillan Center for International and Area Studies. I would like to extend my thanks to the Luso-American Development Foundation (FLAD) and the Portuguese General Directorate for Books, Archives and Libraries (DGLAB), which generously awarded me a fellowship to research physically at the Lisbon National Archive of Torre do Tombo (ANTT). Unfortunately, my trip was not possible because of the start of the pandemic.

Parts of this book were presented in conferences and debated with colleagues from many parts of the world. I can highlight the conferences and symposiums at the University of Kansas, the Yale

Gilder Lehrman Center, the Society of Architectural Historians International Conference, the Architecture of Slavery Symposium in Charleston, and the Lapidus Center Conference. I am especially thankful for Nathaniel Walker and Rachel Engmann for inviting me to publish a chapter in their book.

I thank the employees and owners of the plantations I visited in Brazil—Freguesia, Vitória, Cajaíba, and D'Água—and in the United States—Monticello, Oak Alley, Whitney, McLeod, and Boone. Our conversations gave me awareness and information that allowed me to better understand the past and the use of plantations' spaces. In Brazil, I am very grateful to the ones who made my visit to the plantations possible: Bernadete Primo (secretary of culture of São Francisco do Conde), Maria de Fátima dos Santos (director of the Wanderley Pinho Museum), and Reinaldo Barreto (Federal University of the Recôncavo of Bahia). There are scholars who must be acknowledge for their assistance: Arivaldo Amorim (School of Architecture of the Federal University of Bahia), Rafael Marquese (University of São Paulo), Wellington Castellucci (Federal University of the Recôncavo of Bahia), and Luiz Cláudio "Cacau" Nascimento.

The archival materials were essential to my research, and I am deeply appreciative of the provision of photographs and maps for use in this book. I am indebted to IPHAN (National Historical and Artistic Heritage Institute) units of Salvador, Cachoeira, and Brasília; IPAC (Artistic and Cultural Heritage Institute of Bahia); APEB (Public Archive of the State of Bahia); the National Archive of Rio de Janeiro; the National Army Archive; the Lisbon National Archive of Torre do Tombo; and Lisbon Arquivo Histórico Ultramarino. My special thanks to their employees, particularly Ana Teresa Gois (IPHAN Salvador), George da Guia and Cátia Lázara (IPHAN Brasília), Marcelo Faria (IPHAN Cachoeira), Tatiana Lopes (National Archive of Rio de Janeiro), and Captain Mauro (National Army Archive); their help was instrumental in obtaining the documents and maps I needed. I am also indebted to the staff of the libraries of the University of Kansas and Yale University who helped with many sources to my research, and my extended thanks to the libraries throughout the United States, which sent me books through interlibrary loans. I am also grateful to the architect Diogo Vasconcellos for sharing with me his knowledge about the Cajaíba Plantation, and the generosity of Carlos Santiago for authorizing me to use his wonderful aerial photographs of the Cajaíba Plantation.

I would like to express my gratitude to the editorial board and my appreciation to Louis A. Pérez Jr. for his kind attention and support since our initial contact and throughout the publication process of this book. I also extend my thanks to the reviewers for their valuable comments and suggestions that helped enhance the manuscript, as well as to John McLeod, Sam Dalzell, and everybody involved in the publication process.

I am grateful to my extended family and Brazilian friends who always sent me positive energy. Special thanks to Jane Lee, Gisele Ferreira, José Carvalho, and Alexandrea Haggerty for visiting the plantation sites with me; João Dannemann, for all the exchange of knowledge; Marta Libório, for welcoming me in her house in Brasília and assisting me at IPHAN. Adriana Quadros and Nanny Assis, your support meant a lot to me. My appreciation to my friends in Lawrence; and to my friends in New Haven, I miss our great time at Jane Snaider's Alston House. My thanks go also to my siblings Josiane, Guilherme, Kleber, and my sister-in-law Milene for their support. A special thank-you goes to my niece Bruna, who always cheers my achievements and has been a constant presence in my life.

I owe my deepest gratitude to my son, Leonardo, for his unwavering belief in me, his patience with my hard times, and his dedication in reading my drafts in the middle of his high school duties. He is my rock and support through everything. This work is dedicated to him and to my beloved parents, Wilma Andrade Meyer and Kleber Cosenza Meyer, who always supported my choices. Unfortunately, they passed away during my doctoral studies. Nevertheless, they will always be with me in my heart and thoughts. Last, I am grateful to the infinite forces of the Universe in their most diverse forms of manifestation for their intervention on my trajectory.

List of Figures and Abbreviations

ABBREVIATIONS

APEB – Public Archive of the State of Bahia

IBGE – Brazilian Institute of Geography and Statistics

IPAC – Artistic and Cultural Heritage Institute of Bahia

IPHAN – National Historical and Artistic Heritage Institute

SPHAN – National Historical and Artistic Heritage Secretary

Chapter One

Spaces of Power and Resistance

Yesterday in Sierra Leone,
The war, the lion hunt,
Idly slept carelessly
Under the tents of amplitude!
Today ... the black hold, deep,
Infected, cramped, filthy,
Having the plague instead of jaguar ...
And the slumber always broken
By the rattles of the fallen,
And the thud of a body overboard.

—CASTRO ALVES, 1868[1]

The strophe extracted from the poem *Slave Ship*, written by Brazilian poet Castro Alves, gives only a brief glimpse of the terror of the Middle Passage. Thousands of people were taken from their homes and forced to work on plantations in the Americas. About four million people[2] arrived in Brazil during the almost 360 years of slavery, of which 35 percent went to Bahia, and most of them ended up working on the sugar plantations in the Recôncavo[3] region. The concentration of large lands in the hands of a few men was a hallmark of the Bahian Recôncavo, this leading economic region in Brazil, propelled by the production of sugar. Economic, social, and political powers were held by a small, wealthy group. Consequently, the form of exploitation of resources, including human beings, imposed more than a productive model. It established a way of life and a lasting, unequal relationship between the groups that formed a new society there. The country still has a cause-and-effect relationship between the misery of the Brazilian rural population and the type of agrarian structure implanted there in the past, whose essential feature is the marked concentration of land in the hands of few families.[4] This also caused the migration of descendants of enslaved people from the northeast to the southeast looking for a better life and work opportunities, but it did not prevent them from continuing to experience exploitation and misfortune.

The legacy of slavery has had a profound impact on the societies of the Americas, and this has been discussed in the humanities and social sciences. However, it is only recently that the field of architecture has begun to engage in these conversations and to consider how the legacy of slavery has shaped the built environment.[5] Social, economic, and political factors influence the way in which our cities, towns, and other built spaces are designed and constructed, and the history of slavery is a significant aspect of these forces. Architecture has the power to both reflect and physically shape the values and beliefs of a society, and by engaging with the history of slavery, architects can help create more inclusive and egalitarian built environments.

Therefore, the purpose of this book is to investigate the role of the built environment of the Recôncavo sugarcane plantations in their inhabitants' behavior. By learning about how the built environment influences people, we can gain insights into how the design and layout of spaces can shape behavior and influence power dynamics. The book also aims to include the Brazilian Recôncavo region in the dialogue about plantation slavery landscapes, as well as to enrich the discussion in the field of architecture. Through the analysis of three important plantations from different centuries, this study shows how the spaces of plantations were used as a means to exert power to control the immense population of enslaved people and how the enslaved people used the same spaces to resist the slavery system. It will contribute to scholarship about how architecture participated in the foundations of an unequal Brazilian society that continues to this day. Finally, as the Bahian Recôncavo region was a pivotal economic center during the transatlantic slave trade, and it is home to a substantial population of African descendants, this work makes a valuable contribution to the field of African Diaspora studies.

Historical Background

The region called the Bahian Recôncavo, Brazilian Recôncavo, or only Recôncavo encompasses the lands around the bigger Brazilian bay, the Bay of All Saints, in the current state of Bahia (Figure 1). The bay, with 56 islands, 1,223 square kilometers (472 square miles) of extension, and 9.8 meters (32 feet) of depth, was named after November 1, the Day of All Saints, when the Portuguese first arrived there. A region with a rich fluvial net and a *massapé* soil[6] suitable for growing sugarcane and many other agricultural products, the Recôncavo has attracted human exploitation since the beginning of the colonization of Brazil.[7] The occupation of the area by Amerindian tribes dates back many centuries before the arrival of the Portuguese in Brazil in 1500. However, it was after the Portuguese colonization that the occupation of the area reached scales never seen before. The sugar plantations made the Recôncavo one of the richest regions of colonial Brazil. Taking advantage of the best that the region offered in terms of resources, topography, and visibility, the sugar mills dominated and modified the local environment, occupying the entire Recôncavo region, making use of the rich hydrography, and erecting magnificent buildings that stood out in the bay's landscape and its interior.

The plantations were mostly self-sufficient and only depended on the external market for some supplies. Besides sugarcane and its products, such as sugar and cachaça (a Brazilian liquor distilled from sugarcane), they also produced tobacco, beans, rice, manioc (cassava), and many other products for their subsistence. The basic social groups that occupied the plantations were the masters and their families, the overseers and drivers, the enslaved people, and some free laborers. The spatial and functional system of the plantation was mostly made up of its basic buildings—the Big House, the chapel, the senzalas (enslaved people's quarters), the house of the overseer(s), and the sugar mill—as well as many other small buildings such as sickrooms, carpentry shops, locksmith shops, storage areas, stables, and corrals.

01 Bahian Recôncavo Region and its micro-regions

Map source: https://doi.org/10.1007/s11250-019-01956-5

SUGARCANE PLANTATIONS

The first sugarcane plantations appeared in Brazil in 1532, following the success of Portuguese sugarcane plantations in Cabo Verde, Madeira, and the Açores Islands. The sugar cycle and African slavery were the two institutions that marked Brazil profoundly due to the intensity with which they influenced the development of the colonial cities, as well as the whole country. Colonial Brazil, and especially Bahia, was an agrarian, patriarchal, and slavery society, commanded by the owners of large plantations distributed along the Bahian Recôncavo, from where they centralized and irradiated their power. The owners of these vast sugarcane plantations influenced society at large and the government as well.

The sugarcane plantations and churches were the main agents in the development of the cities in the Recôncavo.[8] The plantations' owners and their families participated in the life of the cities in many ways. Besides building houses and living there part of the year, they helped improve the local commerce, occupied political offices, and supported churches in their religious celebrations and services, promoting and organizing events and donations.

The abundant fluvial drainage of the Bahian Recôncavo, and the location of the capital, Salvador, on a peninsula, facilitated the real possibility of using the fluvial maritime route as the main pathway for regional circulation. This was probably the main reason they built the first settlements precisely in places where it was possible to connect to the waterways.

During the eighteenth century, sugar commerce passed through a crisis in the international market, losing its main place to the gold discovered in the Minas Gerais region. However, sugar retook its place in the colonial economy due to the industrial revolution and the political and social conflicts in the English and French colonies. After Santo Domingo's insurrection in 1791, the Brazilian sugar commerce was reborn, and the plantations grew faster and richer than in the first centuries of the colony.[9] To support this growth, thousands of enslaved Africans were brought in the nineteenth century to work on the Recôncavo sugar plantations. It is estimated that from 1800 to 1850 almost 2,200,000 enslaved people arrived in Brazil.[10]

The cities were the way for the Portuguese Crown to control a colony with vast lands. Through the cities' governments, Portugal controlled the economy of the production and protected the land against pirate attacks. In addition, from the beginning, political power was linked to the Catholic Church, which helped control the population. Because the economic domination came from the rural areas, mainly from the plantations, the formation of the cities was compounded by their urban spaces and all the surrounding plantations that together with the Catholic Church controlled the colony.

CATHOLIC CHURCH

The number and size of religious buildings in the Recôncavo show the importance of the Catholic Church during the colonial period. Not only in the villages and towns, almost all plantations had a chapel to "educate" enslaved people and support the masters and their families. Every urban space had one or more chapels or churches, depending on the number of people living there. The presence of religious buildings indicated territorial expansion. The religious buildings were also a place for social meetings, such as Masses, baptisms, and weddings.[11] Whether it was in the chapels of the plantations or in the main churches of the cities and villages, attending Sunday Mass and religious parties were a ritual for everybody. Even enslaved people had to attend.

The Catholic Church played a very important role in the control and stability of the colony. The Church not only owned many lands, plantations, and enslaved people, but it was also a symbol of the sugarcane plantations because they were inside every plantation of the Recôncavo region. Initially, the priests, mainly Jesuits, catechized the Native peoples, converted many of them to Catholicism, and compelled them to work for the Portuguese in the colonization of the "new" lands. The Indigenous peoples were the first enslaved people working on the plantations. Later, their numbers diminished due to many diseases and wars they waged against the Europeans. Moreover, the Jesuits started to oppose the enslavement of the Amerindians; hence, the Portuguese brought enslaved Africans to work on the sugarcane plantations.

Religion was used to control enslaved Africans by convincing them that their enslavement was a sin and that they would have a better life after death. The religious space had the symbolic force of resignation to convince Black people that they were inferior. Nevertheless, many times the priests fought for some enslaved people's rights, such as allowing them to rest on Sundays and holidays, and sometimes they would even intervene against severe punishments.

The Portuguese were very religious, and the planters had different ways to demonstrate the extent of their faith. For example, they regularly donated money to support the churches of nearby villages, they built spaces on the plantations for the inhabitants to worship, and many times priests lived on the plantations. Some churches were in buildings separate from the Big Houses, others were in buildings attached to the Big House, others were chapels inside the house itself, and the simplest were just altars reserved in some part of the house. Other aspects that show the importance of the churches were the materials used to build them—built-in masonry of stone and other durable materials. Because of this, church buildings have survived to this day on many plantations.

At the end of the eighteenth century, the Recôncavo was one of the most densely populated regions in Brazil. Africans were bought to Bahia to work in many different fields, but the sugarcane plantations were the main focus of their work. Sugar exports increased around 400 percent during this time. Between 1789 and 1800, Bahia exported an average of 12,145 tons of sugar per year. In the period between 1850 and 1855, it reached more than 56,675 tons per year on average. This growth was linked to an increase in the forced African Diaspora, which brought nearly 410,000 Africans to Brazil from 1786 to 1851.[12] To better understand the composition of the Recôncavo inhabitants and their social relations, it is essential to comprehend the economic context outlined by the sugar commerce in the nineteenth century. It was a region that relied heavily on enslaved labor for a long duration of time, and the predominance of Africans and their descendants strongly influenced the culture of the region.

MAIN PRODUCTS

Sugar was always the main product of the Recôncavo region; however, tobacco and cassava were two other important products. Together with the sugar, they helped create a "social and economic landscape"[13] that, alongside slavery, shaped what the Recôncavo became.

Sugar

Sugar was the richest product of the Recôncavo. The cane production was diverse: sugar, molasses, liquor, and so forth. The products were exported from the port of Salvador, however, some were sent to the local market, mainly brown sugar and liquor. In the regions where sugarcane cultivation was possible, sugar plantations became a remarkably stable way of life despite a long history of prosperous times interspersed with depressions. It was an important product in the development of cities and provided support to the inhabitants.[14] In addition, the production of sugar was responsible for a typical social organization, centered on the relationship among the masters of the sugarcane plantations, their families, the enslaved people, and others, such as the overseers, the priests, and some peasants who also lived on many plantations. This shows how the owners of the plantations might have influenced the city and society.

Tobacco

Between 1780 and 1860, the Recôncavo produced a large amount of the world's tobacco, which was the second most important product in economic and exportation value coming from the region. The Recôncavo was the second highest tobacco-producing region in the world. Small farms cultivated these crops, mainly located in the region near the village of Cachoeira and the Paraguaçu River on lands that had twenty to forty enslaved people. Around 87 percent of the tobacco exported to Lisbon came from Bahia. In addition to exportation to the European market, tobacco was used to trade for enslaved people in Africa.[15]

Manioc (Cassava)

Manioc[16] was an important product for the subsistence of the population of the Recôncavo because it was easy to grow and prepare. The production of manioc flour not only went to the local market but was also utilized for consumption on long maritime trips, besides being exported to Portugal and other parts of the Portuguese empire. Peasants cultivated manioc on their small farms for their own consumption and to sell in local and nearby markets. It was usually cultivated alongside products like sugarcane and tobacco.[17] Regarding the local market, smacks and launches were used to transport and trade manioc between the ports along the bay.[18] The regional urban formation had the power to stimulate a substantial demand of local products.

WORKFORCES

Enslaved people were, without doubt, the main labor force in the Recôncavo region. However, there were also groups of rural producers, farmers, and peasants whose work was also important for commerce. The network derived from the production of sugar, tobacco, and manioc linked sugarcane planters, enslaved people, peasants, small farmers, and urban consumers to the local and external markets.[19] Some of these connections also helped enslaved people in their resistance to the slavery system.

Enslaved Africans

Enslaved people were Brazil's most valuable assets, and a man's wealth was measured by how many he had. Enslaved people were an essential part of the economy, as they were one of the bases for the success of sugar commerce. Without them, the history of Brazil would be very different. Brought to work on the sugarcane plantations, in a time when sugar monoculture ruled the colony's economy, Africans contributed not only to the success of this business but also to Brazilian culture, architecture, and urbanization. This study does not intend to extensively analyze slavery and its social and economic variables, which have already been widely studied by many scholars.[20] The purpose is to identify enslaved people's role in the construction/maintenance of plantation spaces, as they were a significant part of the colonial society and had imperative importance in the colonial economy. Besides being regarded as an important commercial product, their commerce stimulated the production and exportation of tobacco to Africa.

Small Farmers, Peasants, and Merchants

Small farmers and peasants were responsible for the subsistence of the local population and for the circulation of their products among small villages and cities. Cassava, generally grown by them, was an extremely important commercial product in the Recôncavo. Some sugarcane slaveholders also allowed enslaved people to cultivate cassava and other small crops on their rest days because it helped them in their own maintenance as well as tied them to the land. Subsistence agriculture and exportation were intimately linked in a complex relationship. The peasantry was directly related to the colonial economy, which arose alongside the slave economy and then grew in importance afterward.[21] It is believed that many small farmers and peasants also had strong social relationships with the neighborhood inhabitants, mainly the enslaved people, which gave them an important role in the configuration of the enslaved people's resistance.

Merchants traveled to plantations, villages, and small cities, selling products from distant locations. They were also responsible for the development of a network of paths to reach remote places, which often were used by enslaved people to escape.

Historical Analysis of Plantation Slavery

LANDSCAPES

The landscapes of plantations in the New World were not simply the result of geographic and cultural conditions. In these landscapes, the territory of confinement and exploitation was achieved through architecture deliberately planned to exert power over enslaved Africans. Research focused on slave societies, whose economies were centered on plantations as a system of production, generally shows a clear spatial organization intended to surveil the enslaved people.[22] The spatial organization of the plantations in the Brazilian Recôncavo region gives the impression that they did not follow the same organization observed in other regions. In the Recôncavo, most plantations seem to have only followed the geography and the topography of the region. Nevertheless, the plantations in the Brazilian Recôncavo also used the built environment to discipline their inhabitants. The research focus of this study is on the contextualization of the relationship between people's behavior and the space on the Brazilian Recôncavo plantations. Like most slave societies in the Americas, the Brazilian Recôncavo plantations[23] constituted a complex place of conditional freedom spatially organized with the purpose of exerting surveillance, discipline, and control over enslaved people's bodies and souls to maximize profits. Those plantations were spaces that restricted the agency of enslaved people. They were organized spaces where people were seen as commodities,[24] in a regime of systemic physical and psychological torture. They used torture as a technology to increase productivity and keep production in operation.[25] This study demonstrates that the oppression suffered by enslaved people was not only a social consequence of slavery but rather a consciously implemented strategy made effective through the planning and construction of plantation buildings. Violence and fear shaped these spaces, and their configurations reveal the power of the oppressive logic of slavery to creatively overcome the most varied types of geography.

An attempt to uncover the use of the spaces in the tense relationship between the Recôncavo plantations' enslavers and enslaved people is what motivated this study. It shows that the control of the built environment on the Recôncavo plantations was essential to the survival of both sides. In this way, this book joins the scholarly debate about how the spatiality of plantations was used in favor of their owners to control enslaved people. The second objective of this study is to analyze how enslaved people reacted, sometimes violently, and rebelled, from the refusal to leave their lands, families, cultures, and histories in Africa, through the rebellions during the harmful Middle Passage, to the most radical forms of rebellion, such as the murder of their enslavers. However, most times the resistance was pacific with the slaveholders barely noticing the intention, such as pretending sickness, breaking tools, or working slowly. Power and resistance are central phenomena for the study of national identities and the perpetuation of the division of classes and ethnicities not only in Brazil but throughout the slaveholding Americas. As discussed by Hegel, what moves social history is the contradiction or opposition between "lord" and "bondsman,"[26] which perpetuates the inequality in the self-consciousness of human beings when different objectives are confronted. Since the beginning of plantation history, two figures were born, the "master" and the "slave," the first imposing on the second the way of work and life, without care for their desires. The second should renounce their desires and recognize the enslaver's power. However, as the power could not be absolute, the enslaved people were able to oppose this imposition and fight against it.

As has been studied in many other regions of the Americas, the landscapes of the plantations were a spatial projection of unequal power relations, a territory defined by the power of those who were in charge and by the submission of those who lived and/or worked there. It resulted from a long process of production and reproduction of a system designed to work based on coerced workforce exploitation. One important element for the vigilance was the location of the overseers' houses. Andrew Wilkins uses historical maps and archaeological excavations not only to link the power with the structure of the plantation spaces, but also to call attention to the importance that the overseers had in the definition of farm spaces. Using some plantation farms in the US South, Wilkins investigates the layouts of overseers' quarters and their relations to enslaved people's dwellings and slaveholders, explaining that the distribution of the buildings took into consideration the surveillance of enslaved people.[27] Similarly, in his arguments about the plantations in Jamaica, James Delle shows that in the layout of coffee plantations, the quarters for overseers were located at strategic points to exert a "panoptic surveillance" on the work and domestic life of enslaved workers, producing a conscious landscape of power.[28] Following Delle's arguments, Theresa Singleton reiterates that the slaveholders manipulated the spatial organization of plantations to restrain and subordinate enslaved workers, aiming to maximize profits through the of use surveillance. After analyzing Cuban coffee plantations, she concludes that Cuban slaveholders acted similarly to most slaveholders throughout the Americas.[29]

In a different way, Felix Haase approaches the analysis from an enslaved person's perspective. Investigating the impact of surveillance on enslaved people through the vision of Frederick Douglass, Haase shows how the surveillance and its production of space affected Douglass physically and psychologically during the time he was enslaved. He argues that slaveholders planned the layout of plantations in a way to control enslaved people and extract work through supervision and physical punishment. Enslaved people internalized the surveillance, which was reflected in their acts; thus, although they could physically cross the plantations' borders, the boundaries created in their minds by the oppression and surveillance often outweighed their desire for freedom.[30]

The manipulation of the built environment was the main form employed to observe enslaved people on plantations. The panopticon concept has been influential in the development of systems of social control, and it has been argued by several scholars[31] (including this study) that some of the ideas behind it were used in the design of slave plantations. It is important to acknowledge that the panopticon should not be analyzed solely in terms of its

physical characteristics as the majority of the time it was its varia-
tions and other arrangements of surveillance that were employed
to underscore the relations of power.[32] According to the panopticon's reasoning, behavior is shaped by a building's design or layout[33]; therefore, bodies in space serve as the platform for power
struggles. Thus, architecture, as an instrument of spatial organization, constitutes an important power mechanism. When discuss-
ing the relationship between power and space, Foucault presents a
conceptual vision of power that includes how it materializes in the
arrangement of physical and social spaces. The structures and out-
comes of power shape and define this arrangement.[34]

BRAZILIAN SUGAR PLANTATIONS

French engineer Louis Vauthier, who worked in Brazil in the nineteenth century, was the first to mention the use of the space to control enslaved workers on Brazilian plantations. Vauthier designed
a plan based on plantations he visited in the state of Pernambu-
co, in which the buildings were arranged around a square, forming
an internal courtyard. The disposition of the buildings helped the
overseers and plantation owners closely surveil enslaved people
and production (Figure 2). Esterzilda Azevedo examines the various
configurations of plantation buildings by comparing iconographies
of sugarcane plantations built in the Bahian Recôncavo between the
sixteenth and nineteenth centuries. Although she made a significant contribution to the study of Bahian plantations, she related the
distribution of the buildings to the sugar production process and
topography, not taking into consideration the power structure.

By studying the complexity of an agrarian society dependent on
enslaved labor, Stuart Schwartz shows the importance of sugar in
the development of the Bahian Recôncavo. Emphasizing the power
relationship between plantation owners and enslaved people,
Schwartz points out that "above all, the nature and organization of
the labor force of the [plantation] determined the pattern of Brazilian society."[35] This was the model followed by later generations and
is still present in Brazilian society today.

As observed by Clifton Ellis and Rebecca Ginsburg, there is a
need for more studies about enslaved people's landscape in Latin

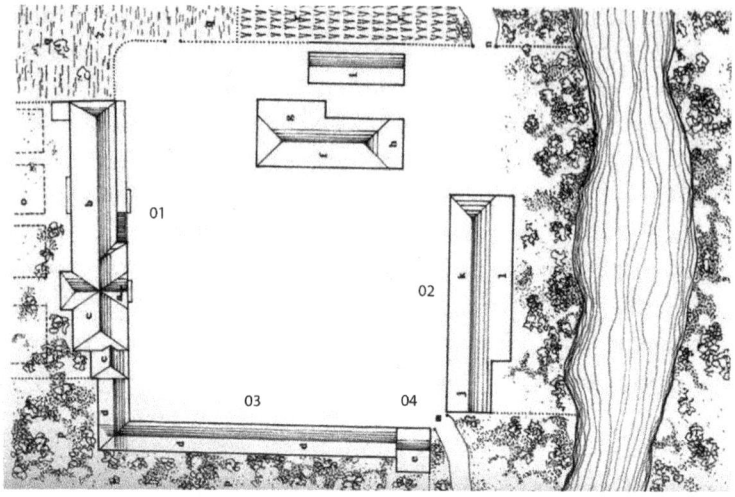

02 Plantation Organization by Louis Vauthier

Plan of a sugarcane plantation designed by Louis Vauthier in the nineteenth century. (1) Big House; (2) mill or center of production; (3) senzalas (enslaved people's quarters); (4) overseers' houses. Louis Vauthier, "Casas de Residência no Brasil," *Revista do SPHAN* 7 (1943): 132.

America to understand the link between the existent sites studied and other ones with similar slave societies such as Brazil.[36] Therefore, the study presented in this book will cover the underexamined use of spatial organization as a tool of control and resistance on the Bahian Recôncavo plantations.

The history of enslaved people's resistance has been repeatedly studied in recent decades to reconstitute a flawed interpretation where, traditionally, enslaved people were seen only as passive agents of a brutal system, when in fact they were effectively transformative agents of their societies. Therefore, during the time of slavery, power and resistance were directly linked because the increase of one led to the increase of the other. To better understand the power used to maintain the system, it is necessary to understand the resistance created against it and vice versa.[37] In a plantation landscape, the same spatial element could be perceived in different ways, like a wall Singleton observed on a Cuban plantation or a fence, as Garrett Fesler suggested. The elements in an environment could awaken different feelings—isolation, protection, confinement, privacy—depending on the point of view of the enslaver and the enslaved person.[38]

Enslaved people reacted against their situation in many ways, sometimes actively but most often through passive resistance. Just as slavery was an intense system, so too were the types of resistance shown by enslaved people to the system imposed on them. Many times, enslaved people used physical and psychological problems as means for skipping work.[39] The forms of resistance could be enacted by individuals or by groups. The most common individual forms of resistance were suicide, abortion, and murder. Many preferred to die rather than remain enslaved. Some women preferred abortion over subjecting their children to the same life of suffering they had experienced. Overseers and even enslavers were killed by enslaved people in reaction to their excessive violence.[40] However, in the midst of enslaved violence, there was almost always a social space where opportunities for bargains arose. The resistance included dancing, singing, establishing religion, sabotaging, and pretending to be sick; all the elements necessary to resist the system were present. With these excuses, enslaved people forged particular political wisdom, reaching spaces for negotiation in the interior of a slave society. Enslaved Africans knew how to deal with the slavery structure, and they tried to break the system in many ways.[41] Enslaved people were a main agent who helped shape the stratification of society. The escapes, sabotages, insubordination, and passive daily resistance constitute the dynamics of the slavery system itself.[42]

Theoretical Framework

SPACES OF POWER

Power is a concept that has been widely used in the social sciences. On plantations, the power dynamic was supported by the legal system, which often did not recognize the rights of enslaved people and afforded them few legal protections. As a result, plantation owners were able to exert a great deal of control over the lives of their workers, and resistance to this power was met with punishment, including physical abuse and legal penalties. This power dynamic was a key aspect of the plantation system and played a significant role in shaping the social and economic relationships that developed on plantations.

Power is a set of historically constructed social practices and discourses that discipline the bodies and minds of individuals and groups. Although physical violence is always a present theme in studies involving the world of sugar, the focus here will be directed more to the functionality of spaces and their use in the maintenance of the dominance and surveillance of the workforce. In fact, the intensity of power and its frequent use represented a fundamental element in the determination of the spatial architecture of plantations and its status as a contingent space of freedom. To the extent that most of the Recôncavo sugarcane plantations belonged to the same families, who also increasingly controlled an enormous number of human lives, the territorial domain of the planters becomes more complete, close, and rigid. Power is like a machine that encompasses everyone involved, both those who exercise power and those who are subjected to it.[43]

PANOPTICON AND DISCIPLINE

According to Foucault, the use of constant surveillance, control, and discipline to exert power on individuals is characteristic of modern social relationships, and the panoptic idea is a way to exert supervision. Foucault calls it a "laboratory of power" to control human freedom.[44] It is a controversial and oppressive approach to social control and has a negative impact on the people subjected to this kind of surveillance. On the plantations, the overseers acted similarly to the panopticon supervisor. They were the authority responsible for surveillance, and therefore, they were usually positioned at a point where they could watch and have a global overview of the plantation structure. Often, the house of the overseer works similarly to the panopticon's central tower.[45] This spatial organization influences the actions of those being monitored in a quite incisive way, once the degree of their visibility induces them to behave according to the norm imposed. The main role of the use of power and disciplinary actions over enslaved workers was to maintain economic production, so the space was organized to extract more work and profit through near, continuous, and regular intimidation.

To keep plantations working as they wanted, overseers needed a disciplinary power that worked directly on the daily lives of enslaved people, maintained not only by vigilance but also by physical punishment. For the control of enslaved bodies, overseers used different punishment mechanisms such as hanging, beating, burning, mutilating, branding, imprisoning, and, the most infamous, whipping. They used these in a space where everybody could see the punished, and even when there was no punishment, the pillory was there all the time, serving as a constant reminder of the price for breaking the system's rules.

Foucault addresses the characteristics and origins of the disciplinary practices of power in *Microfísica do Poder* and reaffirms that these techniques were not invented in the eighteenth century, but rather that they diffusely emerged earlier, in some practices and specific institutions; they were just reelaborated in the eighteenth century and subsequently became hegemonic. Among institutions where diffuse practices of disciplinary power originated, such as spaces for the mentally ill and military organizations, Foucault also includes "large slave companies in the colonies,"[46] which used a similar spatial organization to attain economic and political purposes.

Discipline and "panopticism" are concepts many times intertwined and linked to power and space. Through disciplinary power, the body becomes the workforce in the production mode. Discipline implies control of time; the body is subjected to time for efficient and quick production. This was the same objective as the punishments. For instance, the objective of public punishments was more to leave an impression on those who saw or learned about the punishment than the effect on the person who was punished.[47] Foucault points out that it is the representation of the disciplinary society that aims for the *docilization* of bodies, which is the culmination of the power. The docile body is useful, disciplined, and, above all, productive.[48]

Pierre Bourdieu's theory of social practices[49] posits that individuals and groups are shaped by the cultural and social structures within which they operate. These structures, or "fields," exert a powerful influence on the thoughts, behaviors, and identities of individuals and groups, and can reproduce and reinforce existing power dynamics. Pierre Bourdieu called this set of mental and practical schemas a "habitus"[50] that guides and influences an individual's actions and perceptions in a particular social and cultural context. Bourdieu argued that habitus is the source of an individual's tastes, values, and ways of thinking and acting. The social and cultural practices of an individual's particular group or class shape and influence their preferences, their behaviors, and the choices they make in life. Most of the time the daily habits shape the way they act.

The plantation system itself can be understood as a field, within which plantation owners and enslaved people operated. Plantation owners occupied positions of power and held significant cultural and economic capital, while enslaved people had very little agency or access to resources. Plantation owners used their economic and symbolic power to shape the social practices of enslaved people, dictating their daily routines, work tasks, and even leisure activities. They also controlled the cultural habits of enslaved people, including their religion and family life. Through these social practices, plantation owners were able to reinforce their own dominance and control over enslaved people and maintain the power dynamics of the plantation system.

Therefore, the plantation system was able to reproduce itself over time by a *habitus* that enslaved people internalized and transmitted through generations. Due to the rigid system and rules imposed on them, sometimes some enslaved people developed an "unconscious understanding"[51] that may have manifested itself in a variety of ways, such as by accepting the notion that they were inferior to their enslavers or that they deserved to be treated as property. Enslaved individuals were also subjected to a system of racial hierarchy that, on one hand, shaped their habitus and their relationships with their enslavers and other enslaved individuals. On

the other hand, it also shaped the way overseers behaved on plantations as they were expected to exert control over enslaved individuals who lived and worked there.

However, similar to what happens with many other forms of
exercising control over others, we must analyze the habits on plantations not only from one side but as a set of actions and reactions.
Therefore, we should not only consider the strategies of power used
on plantations to control enslaved people but also the strategies of
resistance used by the last to survive within the oppressive system.[52]

SPACES OF RESISTANCE

John Vlach starts *Back of the Big House* by pointing out that
studying plantation landscapes without Black people's perspective
is "inadequate" and "futile," as the enslaved people's landscape is
not only a reaction to the enslavers' landscape but a strategy to survive the slavery system.

Thomas Ewbank, during his visit to Brazil in the nineteenth century, heard from a Bahian planter that "the slaves are badly fed,
worse clothed, and work so hard that the average duration of their
lives does not exceed six years."[53] While enslaved people were a
valuable source of labor and were used to produce goods and services in high demand, they were also treated as a commodity by a
system that tried to withdraw all their dignity as human beings with
whips, rapes, and flogs. Consequently, the forced diaspora and the
cruelty used to maintain the order on the plantations also provoked
the resistance of enslaved people.

Public and Hidden Transcripts

Most enslaved Africans were not passive in the face of the violence they were subjected to. Many times, even when they demonstrated an apparent submissive behavior—"public transcript"—
they acted in various ways to resist the system. Small acts of
resistance are usually used by marginalized groups in order to
push back against oppressive systems or structures. These acts are
often subtle and hidden, and they can include tactics such as foot-
dragging, sabotage, absenteeism, and evasion. James Scott argues
that these small acts of resistance—"hidden transcript"—can be

effective in challenging power and can have a significant impact on social and political change.[54]

Scott's concept of the public transcript and hidden transcript can be used to understand the behavior of enslaved people in a number of ways. In general, enslaved people were expected to adhere to the public transcript of the slavery system, which involved performing labor and demonstrating obedience and deference to their enslavers and other authorities—for instance, enslaved mothers who taught their children to please their masters to remain safe.[55] Yet, many times the public transcript was enforced through punishment and coercion, and failure to adhere to it could result in harsh consequences. Consequently, enslaved people developed their own hidden transcripts as a way of resisting and challenging the power dynamics of the slavery system. These hidden transcripts could take various forms: feigning illness, foot-dragging, sabotage, absenteeism, and small escapes during the night. These hidden transcripts were usually informal and covert, as enslaved people had to be careful not to draw too much attention to themselves or their actions. These small acts of resistance can be effective in challenging power and can have a significant impact on social and political change.[56]

Unhidden Acts of Resistance

Most of the enslaved people who arrived in the Recôncavo region were from Central Africa, such as the Hausas, Mande, and Fulas, and many of them spoke Yoruba. Hence, besides being united by the same situation of suffering, language and religion were the first common points among many Africans. However, they had problems with Criollos, enslaved people born in Brazil. Many documents show that Criollos did not like the Africans, because they did not understand why they wanted to return to Africa or why they provoked many revolts. Criollos preferred the small daily negotiations with their enslavers. This was demonstrated in a document produced by Criollos during an uprising on the Santana Plantation. One of their requests to return to the plantation was that the enslaver should give the hardest work to the Africans, showing that the Africans were not together with them in the escape and negotiation.[57] This episode also shows that enslaved people's power of resistance could not be ignored. Enslavers, despite having considerable power in the relationship, were also dependent on enslaved people's labor.

Moreover, despite the process of domination, the expropriation of their human condition, and the violence suffered by enslaved people, one can recognize different forms of resistance. They could be individual or collective, and the most visible was escaping.

On several occasions, escapes were provoked by differences between the enslavers and enslaved people. These could be caused by several reasons, the most recurrent of which was when the enslaver broke a previous negotiation or after the enslaved person had undergone severe punishment, which could lead to the flight and formation of *quilombos* (maroon settlements). The quilombos were not always premeditated; in fact, many were spontaneous formations. However, once they existed, other enslaved people could flee to join them.[58]

Furthermore, sometimes escapes were carried out individually. These fugitives often sought shelter in the residence of known freedmen (manumitted) or free men, traveled to another region, or settled in peripheral areas of the city. In order to avoid arrest, escaped enslaved people pretended to be freed Black people performing some type of activity for their survival and being part of the urban peripheral daily life. The mobility of enslaved people around neighboring areas and the knowledge of the spaces of the plantation made the resistance of enslaved people possible. The known paths, the woods inside plantations, and some knowledge beyond their limits were used for the resistance of enslaved people.[59]

Quilombos

The formation of quilombos was one of the most important expressions of resistance. Most of them were not very isolated, so they could interact with society, commercializing their agricultural production with the help of small traders, farmers, and even other enslaved people. Nonetheless, similar to the hinterland maroons in North America, some *quilombolas* preferred building their settlements in isolated areas near a source of clean water and with cultivable soil. However, although the ideal place would be in total isolation, they still needed to trade or appropriate some items from the neighboring towns.[60]

Despite being located in "protected places," most of the time quilombola communities were found in the vicinity of plantations, towns, and cities, where it was possible to maintain ties and create a support network around shared interests. This involved enslaved, free Black, and even White people, from whom they received information about the movement of troops and other strategic matters related to the guarding and defense of communities.[61]

Quilombos represented a world within the broader universe that was the colonial slave society. They maintained a complex relationship that included not only thefts from farms and escape organizations, but also exchanges of stolen products or foodstuffs produced in the quilombos for favors, transport, and other types of facilitation that free men could provide.

The most famous quilombo was Quilombo dos Palmares.[62] Although it was recognized as the largest and most long-lived of Brazilian quilombos, Palmares did not constitute the standard for these agglomerations of runaway enslaved people, which were usually small and used only to escape for a small period of time, a *petite marronage*. However, not everybody living in the quilombos was a runaway enslaved person. There were also freeborn, Indigenous, and sometimes White people. For example, Quilombo dos Palmares had a large number of people born during its sixty years, including its famous leader Zumbi.[63]

As quilombos started to appear in increasing numbers and different places, the repression increased at the initiative of plantation owners, who sent *capitães-do-mato* (slave hunters)[64] in search of fugitives. There were also government initiatives, with military expeditions and more stringent laws. Highway robbery, cattle rustling, raiding, and extortion were just some crimes committed by fugitive enslaved people. Many times, the intention was to undermine the social order.[65]

Buraco do Tatu was the most well-known quilombo in Bahia (Figure 3). It was built in the eighteenth century on the border of Salvador. In 1763 the government discovered the hidden settlement and destroyed it.[66] One can observe in Figure 3 the arrangement of

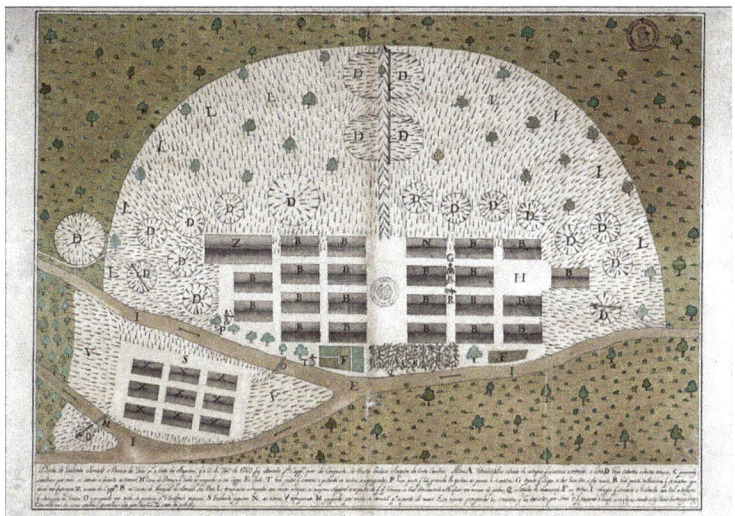

03 *Quilombo Buraco do Tatu*

Plan of Buraco do Tatu quilombo, Salvador, Bahia, ca. 1764. Arquivo Histórico Ultramarino, Lisbon.

the settlement, the cabins uniformly distributed, and the demarcated agricultural spaces. All these elements show a well-organized society with a structure similar to some African tribes, expressing a cultural resistance.

Quilombos were a permanent process of social transformation that expressed the class struggle in the enslaved context. *Marronage* represented a continuous wear-down of the political and economic forces of the slavery system, characterizing it as a revolutionary resistance capable of eroding the stability of the system at its bases. João Reis points out that quilombos represented a symbolic threat, creating nightmares for the enslavers and harassing the slavery system. However, these communities did not aim to demolish the system; most of them only wanted to live well near plantation borders.[67]

Revolts

In addition to the formation of quilombos, when the oppression was very high, enslaved people often joined in revolts against enslavers or overseers. Around 1789, on the Santana Plantation, some enslaved people murdered the sugar master and fled to the forest. Thereafter, they wrote to the plantation's owner a "Peace Treaty," demanding, among other things, better working conditions, permission to cultivate their crops, and the right to rest, play, and sing without permission. In the end, their strategy failed as the slaveholder, pretending to accept the negotiation, captured and punished the rebel enslaved workers. However, their action shows that enslaved people were not resigned to their lives.[68]

Most enslaved revolts in Bahia occurred in the nineteenth century. The strongest revolts were provoked by the Muslim Hausas in 1814 and 1835. The majority of the Hausas came from the Bight of Benin, a very unstable region because of the constant holy wars to expand Islam. The Hausas brought to Brazil their organization and religious wars. In addition, they had a remarkable capacity for resistance. In 1835, the Hausas planned to take the city of Salvador and kill all non-Muslims. They organized this rebellion and planned to carry it out on the last day of Ramadan; however, their organization was betrayed by one enslaved person, and the police put the revolt down.[69] The number of revolts in that century had many factors, including a high number of Africans arriving in Salvador due to the boom of the sugarcane since the end of the eighteenth century, a brutal work environment that included sixteen to eighteen hours of labor a day, and a culture of torture and negligence. All this made enslaved people very unsatisfied.

Spatial Analysis

MOBILITY

From the point of view of the uses of the plantation space as resistance, mobility is an important point in the discussion of fugitive enslaved people. In order to stay away from their enslaver's property and avoid capture by the police or capitães-do-mato, enslaved people had to move and choose places to hide. It was not rare for them to hide in the areas of the plantation itself in places where there was no more planting and the vegetation had grown. They appropriated a space that was relatively seldom frequented and supervised by overseers or drivers.[70] They tested the spatial boundaries of the plantations in small ways by leaving tools out in the fields.

Enslaved people were aware of the limitations of their slaveholders' control and used this knowledge to plan their escapes. They were able to navigate the plantation landscapes and resist surveillance through spatial discipline, even in environments with similar structures of panopticon surveillance. All forms of resistance had only one objective: enslaved people wanted to have agency over their lives.

COGNITIVE GEOGRAPHY

Enslavers used the geography of plantations in their favor to maintain dominance and exploit the workforce. Surveillance and restrictions of movements were applied to enslaved people. The spaces were manipulated to highlight the social and racial differences. All these limits had the main objective of making enslaved people feel inferior and making them easier to control.[71] The built environment evolved into a spatial form of dominance under the influence of the dominant ideology. Life in the interior spaces of plantations was framed by a geography of limited mobility, restricted freedom of enslaved workers, and isolation, all of which facilitated the use of physical force as a way to increase profits.

Analysis of the spatiality of plantations shows that the dominion over enslaved people passed mainly through the control of the productive space, the visibility of the domestic areas, and the circulation of enslaved workers in the landscape. However, the use of the same geographic elements could be extremely important to the resistance actions of enslaved people. The enslaved and the enslaver perceived the geography in different ways. Therefore, panoptic structures of the landscape were not limited to the intentions of their enslavers, but they were also spaces of resistance in the face of the devices of surveillance and control. For example, from the enslavers' perspective, a wall could be used to enclose enslaved people; however, enslaved people could take advantage of the wall to do forbidden activities without being seen.[72]

Enslaved workers either passively or aggressively challenged the command imposed over them through the landscape and appropriated the spaces of the plantations for their interests. There were two ways enslaved people moved through spaces: allowed and forbidden movements. Allowed movements usually occurred when an enslaved person was sent outside the plantation to perform a service for the enslaver, or even for their own interest, but with a permission pass to go out. Nevertheless, the permission pass did not allow them to go wherever they wanted. The types of tasks in the production system and the degree of reliance determined who could leave the plantations and for how long, which determined the kind of movement the person could have. The forbidden movements were going out at night or even escaping for some days (petite marronage), when the enslaved person did not have the intention to run but only to take some time away. However, unauthorized mobility usually ended in punishment. On the Solomon Northup Plantation, a woman was whipped only because she went to a neighboring plantation without authorization to take a soap bar.[73] Hence, when enslaved people decided to carry out an unauthorized activity, they had to be conscious of its consequences.

The "rival geography" developed by enslaved people as a form of resistance to their bondage was characterized by an alternative mapping of the plantation space, including "quarters, outbuildings, woods, swamps, and neighboring farms."[74] Enslaved people expressed themselves in terms of their neighborhood, which meant beyond the plantation itself. The neighborhood was a "joining place" where enslaved people were able to develop "collective identities."[75] For this reason, enslaved people developed, in their daily practices, behaviors that violated mobility control. They escaped the vigilance many times mainly to circulate among the neighboring plantations and villages. Hence, despite the risks inherent in this endeavor, many enslaved people did not fail to meet with enslaved people from other properties, and the local community acquired social and geographical significance to them. However, the enslaved community could be disrupted at any moment as individuals could be sold or relocated to a different place. This required enslaved people to connect with new people. They "were in a constant state of making, remaking, and becoming,"[76] which was important for the development of Black consciousness to help each other survive and keep their culture alive in a system that always tried to kill it. Every neighborhood served as both a place of kinship and discipline. Even with the tight control maintained by the capitães-do-mato outside the plantations, the discipline inside of it, and many other forms of control, enslaved people always created a way to subvert the system.

The importance of considering space as a component present in slave social relations is that it allows one to "see" the subjects and their movements and strategies of power and survival. Considering space as a component that enslaved people took into account means understanding how they questioned and resisted the daily oppression. The enslavers used the landscape to support the racialization. However, outside the plantations, a structure of paths and places created by enslaved people produced a movement environment, a "neighborhood" in which enslaved individuals and runaways joined secretly in a "network of cabins"[77] often built behind the plantations.

The plantation, the quarters, and the forest were the spaces where enslaved people used to transit in either allowed or forbidden movements. Plantations were like prisons because they were where enslaved people lived, worked, and died, and they were always under the authority of an enslaver, subjugated by the whip of the overseer. When they were not in the production facilities or the cane fields, they were usually in their quarters without any privacy as they were usually housed with other people, often sharing a single room. Nevertheless, it was there that Africans from different ethnic groups managed their differences, recreating cultures that were built on sharing experiences that threatened their very existence.[78] Lastly, the forest is usually the place where enslaved people went when they decided to run or hide for some period of time. When runaways were captured, they were treated with extreme cruelty, and the physical punishment that every recaptured fugitive was subjected to depended on the intensity of the anger of the slaveholder or the overseer. Some enslaved people were forced to work with heavy tools around their neck or ankle, some were mutilated, some were held in the pillory for days, and some were killed to serve as an example to others. Even so, the history of escapes was being built throughout the period of slavery.

SPATIAL ANALYSIS OF THE RECÔNCAVO PLANTATIONS

In Brazil, where few plantation records have survived, this study focuses on the existent documents about a few important plantations. This study also extensively uses archival blueprints and physical observation of the plantations' sites and boroughs, including neighboring quilombola communities, which are settlements formed mostly by the descendants of enslaved people.

During colonial times, the Recôncavo encompassed the cities of Salvador, São Francisco do Conde, Santo Amaro da Purificação, Cachoeira, Maragogipe, Jaguaripe, and the vicinities around them. Initially, plantations were established near Salvador, the capital of the colony. By the end of the nineteenth century, with the gradual expulsion of Indigenous peoples, sugarcane plantations were being built along the Paraguaçu River, near where the cities of Cachoeira and São Félix later grew. They were also being built in areas near the Serigi and Subaé rivers, later giving rise to the towns of São Francisco and Santo Amaro. Unfortunately, most of the plantation buildings that existed in the Recôncavo left neither vestiges nor records in books or reports. Some were burned by Indigenous peoples in acts of revenge, others were destroyed by the Dutch, by time, or by economic difficulty; as a result, most of them disappeared,[79] and those that remain are mostly in ruins. Therefore, for a better investigation of the use of space and the built environment, the initial research looked at three factors: (1) which plantations still have the main buildings or parts of them; (2) which plantations had enough documentation in the archives to help in the analyses; and (3) among the ones that filled the first two requisites, which ones were historically or economically important for their time.

After the initial analysis, I chose three plantations from different subregions: (1) Freguesia, a sugarcane plantation from the region surrounding Salvador; (2) Cajaíba, a sugarcane plantation from the region near the Sergipe and Subaé rivers; and (3) Vitória,

04 Map showing the three plantations

Map of the Recôncavo region showing the location of the three plantations, ca. 1830. (1) Freguesia; (2) Cajaíba; (3) Vitória. Dots, numbers, and circles added by the author. Map by Joao Teixeira Albernaz. Rio de Janeiro National Archive.

a sugarcane plantation from the region along the Paraguaçu River (Figure 4).

This book unearths a breadth of diverse archival materials and photographs to explain how the built environments were used on the Recôncavo plantations. Most of this material has never been used by other scholars, and little has been explained in detail in the literature on the history of the Bahian Recôncavo from an architectural viewpoint.

Chapter Conclusion

For decades, slavery has been the subject of research by historians. The topics involving enslaved Africans have become one of the most dynamic of the historiographical production in the humanities and social sciences. Despite this, many questions involving slavery continue to await answers, mainly in the field of architecture in which studies have only recently begun to appear. This study involves a work of research, interpretation, and organization of information relative to the Brazilian Recôncavo region during the African slavery period (1536–1888).[80]

Having framed the theoretical and historical background, the next chapters will examine the region in more detail by providing an analysis of three of the most important plantations of the Recôncavo, plantations whose families were among the most influential economically, socially, and politically in the region. The analysis of these plantations shows that the enslaved people there and most of their freeborn descendants were subjected to social norms designed to maintain a social hierarchy. On one hand, these plantations had different geographies and ways to surveil and punish enslaved people. On the other hand, enslaved workers found a variety of ways to resist the system.

With this proposal, this work is structured in five chapters, including this introductory chapter and the epilogue. In this chapter, the theoretical references are explained, and the spatial and temporal cuts are chosen. The chapter also identifies the region and explains its importance for the development of the country. The objective of the chapter is not to explain in detail the theories and history of the region, as there is a vast scholarship about this. Rather, the aim of the chapter is to contextualize the theories and locate the region in time and space, and the socioeconomic factors of the period investigated. The next chapters show that power and resistance are always intertwined.

Bourdieu's concept of habitus helps explain how social structures and power relations shape individuals' habits, dispositions, and ways of acting and thinking. Both Foucault's panopticon and Scott's hidden transcript can be seen as examples of how this process takes place, with the panopticon serving as a means of disciplining and controlling individuals' behavior, and the hidden transcript representing a way for individuals to resist and subvert these power relations.

Chapters 2, 3, and 4 present a temporal analysis of three plantation sites in Brazil: the Freguesia Plantation from the sixteenth century, the Cajaíba Plantation from the eighteenth century, and the Vitória Plantation from the nineteenth century. The analysis of each plantation focuses on the following aspects: (1) the overall spatial organization of the plantation, including the location of the main buildings—Big House, sugar mill, overseer's house, and senzalas (enslaved people's quarters); (2) the functionality of each main building, embracing how they were used within the overall functioning of the plantation and the way the buildings were connected and interacted with the others; (3) the use of the built environment for discipline, including an examination of the ways in which the physical layout was used for surveillance, punishment, and separation; and (4) the resistance of enslaved people through the use of plantation spaces. This last aspect involves an examination of the ways in which enslaved workers used the physical spaces of the plantation to resist and subvert the system of slavery, such as through the creation of secret meeting places or the appropriation of resources for their own benefit. Overall, these four areas of analysis provide insight into the ways in which the architecture and design of the plantation system in Brazil were used to exert control and exploit enslaved workers, as well as the strategies employed by enslaved people to resist and subvert the system.

The analysis of the three plantations covers the entire period of slavery in Brazil, which started in the middle of the sixteenth century and was abolished in 1888. Nonetheless, it was observed during the investigation process that although the plantations started production in different centuries, the main buildings and the spatial organization were from the eighteenth and nineteenth centuries. Thereafter, in order to keep up with the transformation both in the built environment and in using the spaces by the inhabitants, the plantations are analyzed in their physical and spatial organization and the use of the landscape for distinct proposes—power and resistance.

The epilogue closes the book by showing the enduring legacies of plantation slavery in Brazilian society and how the architecture of plantations still influences the contemporary architecture of Brazilian cities and residences. Many Brazilian homes and neighborhoods still have a hierarchical layout, with the wealthier residents living in larger, more luxurious homes and the poorer residents living in smaller, more modest homes or in favelas, which are informal settlements that often lack basic infrastructure and services. The legacies of plantation slavery are also evident in the way that Brazilians from different classes and ethnicities relate to each other. There is often a marked divide between the wealthy and the poor, and between those of European descent and those of African or Indigenous descent. This can be seen in the way that different groups live, work, and socialize, as well as in the levels of access to education and other resources.

Chapter Two

Freguesia Sugarcane Plantation

The slaves are the hands and feet of the owner of the plantation, because without them in Brazil it is not possible to build, repair, and expand the plantation, nor have a working sugar mill.

—ANDRÉ JOÃO ANTONIL, 1711[1]

Introduction

Freguesia, which is among the oldest plantations in Brazil, was a highly productive plantation in the Recôncavo region. Freguesia's Big House, together with the chapel, is one of the most remarkable monuments of the Recôncavo region (Figure 5). The building now houses the museum of the Recôncavo Wanderley Pinho, preserving the history of a region that witnessed the formation of a nation with strong, mixed, and rich ethnic roots. Its surroundings, which are considered a natural heritage, are constituted by a large area with a varied topography, formed by several caves, ponds, and mangroves.

Gabriel Soares mentioned the buildings of the Freguesia Plantation when he traveled through the Recôncavo in 1587. Hence, the plantation dates back to the 1560s,[2] which was also the beginning of the flourishing of the sugar economy in the Recôncavo region. In the oldest geographic maps of the Recôncavo, it is possible to identify the Freguesia Plantation, which sometimes goes under the name of Caboto or Matoim.[3] Freguesia and other nearby plantations operated throughout the slavery period, from the sixteenth to the nineteenth centuries. Although the Big House and the chapel are safely kept by a historical heritage authority (IPAC), the complex was in critical condition during my visit in 2019. In 2020 the government started the renovation of the current buildings and the recovery of the destroyed ones.[4]

05 Freguesia Plantation Big House and Chapel

Freguesia's Big House and Our Lady of Piedade Chapel, 1943.
Photo by Silvanísio Pinheiro. IPHAN Archives.

The Region: Candeias and Caboto District

Freguesia is in the district of Caboto on the shore of the Bay of All Saints. Caboto belongs to the municipality of Candeias, which is integrated into the Metropolitan Region of Salvador and the Recôncavo region (Figure 6). In the sixteenth century, the Portuguese did not find any precious stones or precious metals like the Spaniards did in Spanish America; hence, they turned their attention to natural wealth and invested in the exploration of pau-brasil wood[5] and sugarcane. Therefore, agriculture determined their first settlements. One of the first areas in Brazil to experience the success of the sugar economy was the Candeias region, which is only forty miles from Salvador.

The history of the formation of Candeias and its urban area is intimately linked to the many plantations that operated in the vicinity of the Freguesia Plantation and the small village of Caboto, whose main activities included the transportation of sugar to the capital. It also included small businesses and fishing. Today Caboto

06 Map highlighting Candeias

The Bahian Recôncavo region. Candeias microregion highlighted by the author. The red dot shows the location of the Freguesia Plantation. IBGE/DGC, 2018.

is a small village of fishermen and receives tourists who visit the beaches and eat local seafood.[6]

During the sixteenth century, from 1560 to 1600, sugarcane commerce was prosperous and growing, although there were many crises in the seventeenth century. The worst was in 1626, during the Dutch invasion of the Bay of All Saints, which destroyed sugar mills and villages. In 1666, there was a great economic depression. The increases in taxes and diseases, and the alteration of the currency caused the expenses of plantations to rise significantly. The beginning of the eighteenth century was a prosperous phase, but the competition with other colonies was strong, making prosperity an illusion. The discovery and exploitation of gold and diamond mines on the southeastern of Brazil, which made everything expensive, especially oxen, horses, and enslaved workers, also aggravated the situation. Only around 1766 was there a real phase of prosperity. Taxes on foods were abolished, and freedom of internal trade was reestablished in the colonies. The adoption of technological advances such as the plow, the introduction of steam-powered machines, and the opening of Brazilian ports to other nations reestablished periods of prosperity for sugar commerce.[7]

History of the Freguesia Plantation

Freguesia was one of the first plantations in Brazil at a time when Portugal was looking to populate the new land, giving many incentives to build plantations. Portugal wanted the plantations' owners to not only build plantations on the shore of the rivers but also to expand the plantations' lands to explore the interior of the colony. The Freguesia Plantation worked for four centuries with few interruptions. It stopped production definitively in 1890, after the abolition of slavery. During his trip through the Bay of All Saints, Gabriel Soares described Freguesia as the Sebastião de Faria Plantation with a large sugar mill, enslaver's house, the Church of Our Lady of Piedade, and many other small buildings.[8] At that time, the Freguesia Plantation did not have the architectural form that it presents today. Its installations were much simpler in the beginning. There are reports that around 1624 the Dutch attacked and burned down the Freguesia Plantation main house and the parish church of Nossa Senhora da Piedade. A few decades later, between the years 1680 and 1690, the plantation was sold to Antonio da Rocha Pita, and it remained in the control of his family for many decades. In 1760, Captain Cristovão da Rocha Pita, one heir and owner of the Caboto Plantation, incorporated the two plantations and rebuilt Freguesia's buildings. It is believed that, at that time, the current configuration of the architectural complex of the plantation was probably delimited. It consisted of a large house and adjoining chapel, in addition to the plantation's other buildings.

With the increase in sugar production around 1817, the old animal milling machines were replaced by steam engines. In 1848, Antonio Bernardino da Rocha Pita e Argolo, the future Count of Passé, acquired the plantation and carried out what would be a significant intervention to restore the architectural complex. In 1877, after his death, the plantation was inherited by his granddaughters Maria Luiza and Antonia Tereza and administered by their father, João Maurício Mariani Wanderley, the Baron of Cotegipe. In 1886, through the marriage of Maria Luiza to João Ferreira de Araújo Pinho, the plantation passed to the Araújo Pinho family, who managed it until its deactivation in 1890. One of their sons, José Wanderley de Araújo Pinho (1890–1967, referred to as Wanderley Pinho in what follows), who was a historian and politician, inherited the Freguesia Plantation and other plantations, which he managed with other heirs.

In 1968, after the death of Wanderley Pinho and due to the plantation's great historical value, the federal government expropriated the buildings for the installation of the Museum of the Recôncavo Wanderley Pinho, paying homage to the historian and former owner. The museum was inaugurated in 1971. As was noted earlier, the museum is being renovated to reopen again to exhibit the history of the Recôncavo sugarcane plantations.

Spatial Organization

The Freguesia Plantation is strategically located near Salvador, in a large cove located in the northeastern part of the Bay of All Saints and in front of Maré Island. According to archival maps, this part of the mainland was where the mouth of the Matoim or Cotegipe River marked the location of the Freguesia Plantation (Figure 7). The plantation covered an area of 1,000 hectares (2,471 acres) and reaches 50 meters (164 feet) of altitude at its highest topographical point. It was endowed with mangroves and rich fauna. The plantation had two fishponds formed by tanks dug into the earth, with a communication channel to the water and one or two floodgates.[9] Vauthier describes that usually "sugarcane fields comprise at least one-fifth of the [plantation] area. The vast pastures on which the animals walk free have an almost equal area. Cassava plantations, a coffee plantation, and some rice fields occupy a minimal part. The rest are woods and vacant land, unsuitable for culture."[10]

The main buildings were distributed near the water a few meters away from each other. Only the church was built attached, to the right side of the house. The sugar mill was on the shore of the bay and had some senzalas on one of its sides. The overseers' houses were located in front of the sugar mill building, between the Big House and other row of senzalas. It is known that the plantation used oxen to move the two milling machines.[11] However, there is no registered information about the location of the corral. It could

07 Hydrographic map showing Freguesia Plantation

Map showing the location of the Freguesia Plantation, ca.
1831–1849. Square added by the author. Rio de Janeiro National Archives.

be assumed that it was close to the sugar mill, as were other significant small buildings—a wood storage area, sickrooms, and more.
Gabriel Souza mentions that the plantation looked like a village.[12]
The Big House and chapel were strategically located on the hill and
close to the other buildings of the plantation (Figure 8). Furthermore, the dominant landscape was the sugarcane crops and woods,
which occupied the lands around the ponds (Figure 9).

Spaces of Power

The architecture of the plantation was not merely built to support sugar manufacturing; it was articulated to optimize production. This meant exploiting enslaved workers to their limits. The
spatial isolation of plantations guaranteed owners an almost absolute control of the interior. The geography of the plantation was

08 Aerial View of Freguesia Plantation

Spatial organization of the Freguesia Plantation's buildings. (1) Big House; (2) chapel; (3) sugar mill; (4) senzalas (enslaved people's quarters); (5) overseer's house; (6) facilities. Rectangles and numbers added by the author. Map Data: Google Earth, Maxar Technologies, 11/14/22.

09 Area of Freguesia Plantation

Approximate area occupied by the Freguesia Plantation until the nineteenth century. Line and names added by the author. Map data: Google Earth, Maxar Technologies, 08/26/20.

used in favor of the plantation owners to maintain the mastery and exploitation of the captive workforce. Life inside the plantations was framed by a built environment whose characteristics aimed to limit mobility, and with that, the freedom of individuals, facilitating the use of physical force as a way to increase profits. For that, each detail of the buildings and how they were located was taken into consideration in two main aspects: discipline and sovereignty.

BIG HOUSE

The four-floor Big House with fifty-seven rooms and a construction area of 1,858 square meters (20,000 square feet) was an imposing building that represented the power and superiority of the owners. It is one of the oldest and most sophisticated exemplars of a plantation's Big House in Brazil. The house has a high monumental value due to the preservation of its main characteristics, such as its typology, volumetry, construction technique, and ornamental elements. Although the first plantations were built by the Portuguese colonists, the architecture of the Big Houses was a Brazilian vernacular architecture appropriated for the new environment.[13] The current house was built around 1760, replacing the old one from the sixteenth century.[14] The construction follows the topography of the terrain in a position to watch the surrounding area (Figure 10).

Due to the topography, the first two floors are only partially built. There was no communication between these two floors or to the other floors of the house, and they were accessed by side doors. The first floor was utilized for storage and probably as a punishment room, as there are still some torture instruments there.[15] On the second floor, there were various rooms, including a vestibule, a storage area, an administrative office, and eight small rooms, which could have been bedchambers for enslaved domestic workers or workers with some privileges such as the sugar master, carpenters, and blacksmith. Some of these rooms may have been for guests who were traveling and needed to spend the night.[16] The third floor, or noble floor, was where the family lived. The domestic environment reflected a power structure that influenced and was influenced by its occupants. One can notice that the Big House was structured to limit and control outside access and the contact of strangers with

10 Big House of Freguesia Plantation
The manor was built in the hillside, 2019. Photo by Doriane Meyer.

members of the family. This third level, where the family lived, had only two entrances, from the sides.

The main entrance was made by the side stairs ending in the landing that gives access to the vestibule as well as to the adjoining chapel. This third floor of the Big House was constituted by a vestibule, a living room (Figure 11), a dining room, a small prayer room, and six bedrooms. The kitchens were toward an internal patio where there were also storage rooms and three small bedrooms outside the private zone, perhaps for guests related to the family, and behind the kitchens, there were two bedrooms for enslaved domestic workers (Figure 12). The fourth floor was where the cleric lived (Figure 13). It was linked to the church's second-floor tribunes. There were three living/dining rooms and four bedrooms. The access to this floor was from three staircases that linked it to the church, the service zone, and the main third-floor hallway. A floor only reserved for the cleric shows the importance of religion for the owners, and they likely used religion to manipulate the enslaved.

11 Living Room of Freguesia's Big House

The living room with fresco painting on the walls, 1943. Photo by Silvanísio Pinheiro. IPHAN Archives.

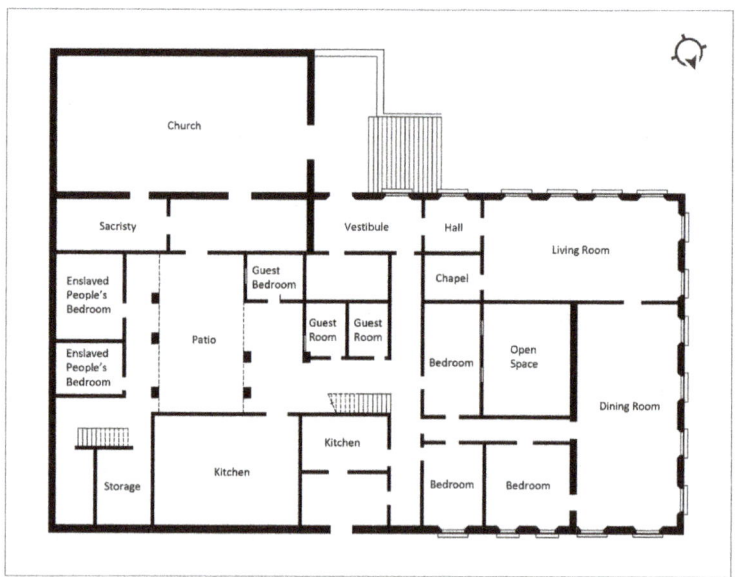

12 Plan of the Third Floor of Freguesia's Big House

The floor where the family resided. Drawing by the author from the plan designed by Jair Brandão, 1944. Original plan courtesy of IPHAN/Bahia.

13 Clerics Rooms at Freguesia

The fourth floor was occupied by the clerics who lived at the Freguesia Plantation. Photo by Doriane Meyer, 2019.

Instead of verandas, similar to some houses of the same period, the house had balconies and two internal patios for better ventilation and illumination. The larger internal courtyard was also used to separate the service area from the social and intimate areas of the family. It is noted by the size of the kitchen that the house probably received a lot of people. The living and dining rooms had sophisticated furniture, and the walls were covered by frescoes with countryside seascapes painted in the renovation of 1856 at the behest of Count Passé.[17]

CHAPEL

The Chapel of Our Lady of Piedade's exact date of construction is uncertain, but a map from 1640 already shows it there, in front of Maré Island (Figure 14). However, due to the destruction provoked by the Dutch, it was probably rebuilt later. Its architecture

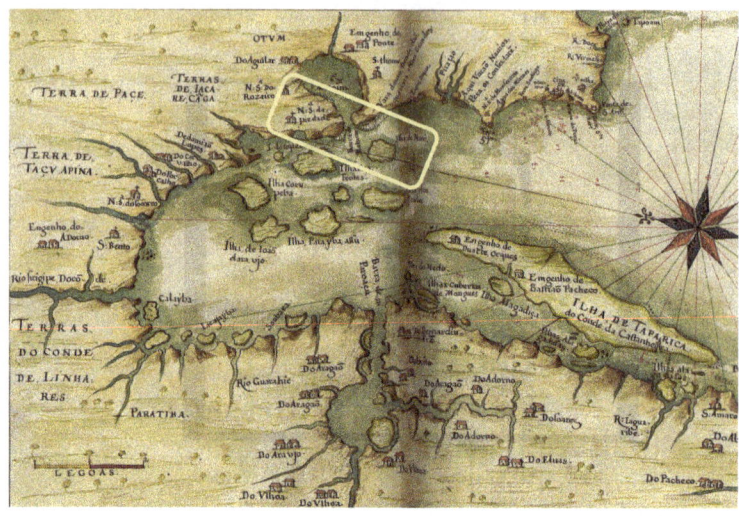

14 Map showing Our Lady of Piedade Chapel

Map of the Bay of All Saints showing Our Lady of Piedade Chapel in front of Maré Island, 1640. Rectangle added by the author. Map by Joao Teixeira Albernaz. Rio de Janeiro National Archive.

15 Our Lady of Piedade Chapel

The chapel's door and the main entrance to the Big House share the same stairway landing, 2019. Photo by Doriane Meyer.

resembles that from the eighteenth century (Figure 15). The construction of the chapel is distinguished by its architectural features and the uniqueness of being combined with the house, with part of the facade embedded in the body of the house with internal access from the third and fourth floors of the Big House—one of the rare exemplars still preserved. It has a narthex, side aisles, chancel (Figure 16) choir space, and tribunes. The ceiling lining features a medallion of Our Lady of Conceição, which was also the name of the private chapel inside the Big House.

An interesting detail is that, different from what happened on many other plantations, the enslaved people here were allowed to watch Mass from the first floor, together with the men from the enslaver's family, relatives, guests, and neighbors.[18]

The choir space located on the second floor was reached either by stairs inside the church or directly from inside the Big House. Women used this space to watch Mass (Figure 17). It has a frontal *mashrabiya* (sometimes spelled "moucharaby") to prevent them from being seen by people from outside the family.[19] These latticework elements were commonly used in Islamic architecture. It was a legacy left by the Arabic culture in Portugal and later transmitted to Brazil. At Freguesia, not only were enslaved people kept under surveillance but White women were as well. At that time, White women, mainly the singles, were kept hidden from visitors' eyes. The space for their use in the chapel was linked directly to the interior of the house. Also, the internal patios on the Big House were used to maintain their privacy.

SUGAR MILL

During the period when the museum was temporarily closed, the old sugar mill building (Figure 18) was completely ruined, leaving only a few walls and pillars (Figure 19) and some objects used in the production of sugar (Figure 20). It was a large L-shaped building with an area of 2,970 square meters (31,968 square feet). The walls of the building were built with brick, and its columns supported the wood structures of the roof covered by clay tiles. The functions of sugar production divided the spaces of the sugar mill: the *picadeiro*, where the cane was stored before being squeezed;

16 Altar of Our Lady of Piedade Chapel

The altar on the chancel of the chapter. IPHAN Archives.

17 Choir of Our Lady of Piedade Chapel

The choir on the second floor where the women watched Mass protected by a mashrabiya, 1943. IPHAN archives.

18 The Sugar Mill at Freguesia Plantation

This façade is oriented towards the Big House, 1943. Photo by Silvanísio Pinheiro. IPHAN Archives.

19 The ruins of the sugar mill

Milling space and the boiler room, 2019. Photo by Doriane Meyer.

20 Original pots used to cook the molasses
Cooper cauldrons used for boiling cane juice, 2019. Photo by Doriane Meyer.

the milling space; the boiler room, with its furnaces; the purging space, where the sugar was separated by quality; and the boxing room, where the sugar was packaged and stored. The only spaces without a wall were the picadeiro and the milling spaces, where there were two milling machines rotated by oxen (Figure 21).[20] One interesting detail at Freguesia was the presence of an elevated platform used by the sugar master to supervise the cooking process of sugar, which could mean closer surveillance over the sugar production to avoid sabotage.[21]

The row of senzalas located on one side of the sugar mill building, shared a wall with the purging space. Close to the sugar mill there was a pier to quickly transport sugar to the port of Salvador by boat.

SENZALAS
"Senzalas," the word for enslaved people's quarters in Brazil, is derived from the Bantu language Quimbundo (or Kimbundu),

21 *The milling machine at Freguesia*
There were two milling machines rotated by oxen. IPAC Archives.

spoken in Angola. It comes from the root "nsala," which means "dwelling" or "place of residence."[22] They were small rooms attached to each other. The architecture of senzalas remained almost the same over the whole slavery period. Of all the buildings on plantations, the most rudimentary were the senzalas. Louis Vauthier described Brazilian senzalas in detail: "Hardly a human habitation could be reduced to a simpler expression. The bare earth constitutes its own floor. The dimensions of each cubicle reach only three and a half square meters ... each of these tight rooms have either a whole family or two or three single people.... It is there where these [enslaved] people live, procreate, get old and die ... severely exploited."[23]

Enslaved people at the Freguesia Plantation lived either inside the Big House (Figure 22) or in the two rows of quarters near the

22 Quarters of the Domestic Enslaved in the Big House

Quarters for domestic enslaved workers inside the Big House with access from the internal patio in front of the kitchen, 2019. Photo by Doriane Meyer.

23 Senzalas at Freguesia Plantation

A row of senzalas (enslaved people's quarters) (right) in the same building as the sugar mill, 1945. IPHAN Archives.

overseers' houses—the one close to the small buildings and the other attached to the sugar mill building (Figure 23). These were ways to closely watch enslaved people. The rudimentary construction of senzalas and spaces for the domestic workers at the back of the house were also ways to show the difference in status and hierarchy.

OVERSEERS' HOUSES

Similar to many plantations, the overseers' houses at the Freguesia Plantation were near the sugar mill and the enslaved people's quarters. With that, they could watch both the production and the enslaved people during the night. The overseers were the eyes of the enslavers.[24] They were responsible for the distribution of labor, the vigilance of enslaved workers, and the coordination of sugar production. They were also the ones who usually punished enslaved people.

The houses of the overseers, like senzalas, were a simple construction. Most of them did not survive the passage of time. They were usually made of wattle and daub (*pau-a-pique* or *taipa-de-mão*, in Portuguese) and covered by clay tiles. The overseers' houses at Freguesia were small constructions with a door, windows on the four sides, and a porch (Figure 24).

Spaces of Resistance

Slavery had a profound impact on Brazilian culture, influencing art, music, religion, and other aspects of society. However, the most deeply rooted aspect was the social relations based on oppression and the introspected or pretended subservient condition of Black men and women to the enslaver. Despite this, this period was not free of conflicts, struggles, disputes, and countless uprisings. Enslaved workers always had strategic actions to resist their confined lives. From small daily resistance to large conflicts, enslaved people sought ways to resist their miserable situation from the beginning. Therefore, notwithstanding the intensity of the spatiality of control, enslaved workers used the same spaces to circumvent

24 The Overseer's House at Freguesia Plantation

The overseer's house (left) located close to the senzalas (enslaved people's quarters), 1945. IPHAN Archives.

the slavery system. Enslaved people developed many means to fight against the system.

DAILY RESISTANCE

According to the census of March 15, 1811, among the list of enslaved people on the Freguesia Plantation, there were "physically disabled, blind of one eye, addicted to fleeing and stealing," showing the acts of resistance and the marks of punishments received for that.[25] Work stoppages, escapes, and revolts were among a variety of forms enslaved people used to fight against the system. However, the most common were the everyday peaceful techniques of resistance. Enslaved people tried to break the domination through small acts of disobedience, personal manipulation, sabotage, and cultural autonomy. Enslaved workers had many ways to create chaos in the daily life of the plantation, such as pretending they were sick, breaking tools, or sabotaging the sugar process. However, many times, they preferred small, unusual behaviors to avoid punishments. The resistance could be subtle but constant, and most of the time this behavior was not noticed by the enslavers/overseers. However, this does not imply an absence of resistance. Among these deeds were food theft, subtle escapes, and poorly performed services.[26] Although enslaved workers could express subservience, they behaved and reacted in ways that allowed them to take advantage of the times they were not surveilled.

When researching the Freguesia Plantation, one can find many subtle ways similar to these examples that enslaved people could have and probably used as covert forms of resistance. Freguesia had a spacious kitchen with four wood stoves (Figure 25), in which an enormous amount of food was prepared for the families, guests, and clerics, so it was easy for enslaved people to steal food. They could also use "witchcraft conspiracies" such as putting small poisonous leaves in the family dinner to cause stomach pain or other diseases. Many enslaved people dominated the use of plants for medicinal uses. They also knew which ones were poisonous. During the time of slavery, some enslaved people killed their enslavers by poisoning them or they used herbs or leaves to provoke pain. For example, in the city of Recife, for three years two enslaved men poisoned their enslaver's milk and other foods.[27]

Enslaved people were not resigned to their lives, and they found many ways to resist the slavery system. However, the search for signs of resistance is often difficult, especially subtle daily resistance. Therefore, the study of enslaved people's resistance, no matter how difficult it may seem, should constitute an important line of research in the study of slavery in the Americas.[28]

On a vast plantation such as Freguesia, with an enormous Big House, extensive landscape, and significant number of workers, many strategies of daily resistance could have been used without notice by the enslavers. Enslaved people on large plantations often had to find subtle ways to resist their oppressors and assert their own agency. These inconspicuous forms of resistance were often necessary in order to maintain a sense of dignity and autonomy in the face of oppressive conditions.

25 The Kitchen of Freguesia Plantation

A 68-square-meter (732-square-foot) kitchen with four wood stoves, 2019.
Photo by Doriane Meyer.

Domestic enslaved people were occasionally granted certain privileges, which allowed for greater freedom of movement. Thus, some were able to escape under the cover of night, particularly on plantations like Freguesia where there was a forest behind the house, providing ideal conditions for them to climb up the hill unnoticed. In addition, enslaved people at Freguesia could probably use the thickets between neighboring plantations to meet and talk safely, not only about ways to resist but to also just unburden about their hard lives.

As Scott calls these small resistances "hidden transcripts," he also points out that "anger, humiliation, and fantasies are always experienced within a cultural framework created in part by offstage communication among subordinates."[29] The domain of hidden discourse is the preparatory space for protest and rebellion. Even though there are no known records of revolts on Freguesia, on a plantation that worked for more than 300 years and passed through

26 An Instrument for Torture

Stocks were used to punish enslaved people on the Freguesia Plantation.
The piece was in the basement of the Big House. Photo by Doriane Meyer, 2019.

27 Nègres ào Tronco Painting

Nègres ào Tronco, painting by J. B. Debret, shows the use of stock in the
plantations. First published in *Voyage pittoresque et historique au Brésil*
(Paris: Firmin Didot Frères, 1834–39), planche 45. Wikimedia Commons.

many generations, without doubt, enslaved people did a variety of
small acts of resistance there. Nevertheless, some were noticed and
punished, as is evidenced by the existence of instruments of torture
(Figures 26 and 27), but certainly many small daily acts of resistance
went unnoticed as well.

As mentioned, there was also a fear of enslaved people sabotaging sugar production revealed by the existence of an elevated platform used by the sugar master to surveil the production and avoid
any damage by enslaved workers.[30] It is an element that was not

commonly found on other plantations. In addition, at the Freguesia Plantation the sugar masters had unusual privileges. They received many gifts, good food, and money as a reward for good production,[31] which undoubtedly included the protection of the production of sugar against sabotage. Therefore, as previously explained, even when enslaved people did not declare an open revolt against their oppressors, this did not imply an absence of resistance. Under the cover of passivity, there were robust invisible acts of resistance that in all likelihood took place.

SIMULTANEOUS SURVEILLANCE

On Freguesia Plantation, the distribution of the buildings implies that enslaved people lived in a system of surveillance and control of the physical spaces where they lived (quarters), worked (mill, cane fields, Big House), and socialized (between the sugar mill and the Big House). On the plantation, in almost all areas they looked, the enslaved could feel the expression of that power. The fence that delimited the plantation, the bell that enforced strict schedules (Figure 28), and the clothes that characterized their captive condition were examples of elements that contributed to the oppression of enslaved people.

At Freguesia the ring of the bell called enslaved people to join the daily count and receive the list of tasks. The bell was also used to call them to Sunday Mass.[32] From the many windows and balconies of the Big House, the enslavers could watch this daily organization, the movements around the mill, and the senzalas (Figure 29). In the same way, the overseer lived close to the senzalas and could observe them, day and night, without being seen. However, on a plantation the size of Freguesia, it was almost impossible to surveil enslaved workers the whole time. There is a hill behind the buildings, and the cane fields were far, which hindered the visual surveillance from a distance.

Additionally, in the same way enslaved people were observed, they could also watch the enslavers' and overseers' movements. From the sugar mill, enslaved workers could see the Big House (Figure 30), and from their quarters they could see both the Big House and the overseer's house (Figure 31). Therefore, when they wanted,

28 The Bell of Freguesia Plantation

The bell located in front of the chapel was used to call enslaved people to work or to Mass. 1943. IPHAN Archives.

29 A view of the mill from the Big House

A view of the ruins of the sugar mill from the balcony of the Big House, 2019. See also figures 18 and 23. Photo by Doriane Meyer.

30 A view of the Big House from the Mill

While working, the enslaved people could observe the Big House. 2019. Photo by Gisele Ferreira.

31 Enslaved views from their quarters

(1) Big House (02) Overseers' house (03) Senzalas. Yellow marks added by the author. Map data: Google Earth, Maxar Technologies, 11/14/22.

enslaved people could take advantage of their own surveillance to escape or do small acts of resistance.

According to inventories of the Freguesia Plantation, in 1811 there were 82 enslaved people, and in 1856 there were 163.[33] These statistics show that no matter how many drivers and overseers were there, the enslaved would largely outnumber them, and so, they could still use the spaces for many acts of subversion, mainly during the night, without being caught.

BRECHA CAMPONESA

Another mechanism for controlling and maintaining the slave order was the creation of an economic margin for the enslaved person within the slavery system, the so-called *brecha camponesa* (peasant breach).[34] It consisted of the assignment of a piece of land (in usufruct) to some enslaved workers and a weekly rest (from plantation work) to work this land.[35] In this way, the enslaver increased the production of foodstuffs that were necessary for slavery, in addition to providing the enslaved with a way to escape the pressures resulting from slavery and attaching them to the land.[36]

A survey about Caboto and Matoim plantations (which belonged to the same family who owned Freguesia) in 1854 talks about lands occupied by "slaves' manioc,"[37] which suggests crops cultivated by enslaved people. When he passed by the Freguesia Plantation, Gabriel Sousa saw people working in small crops near the sugar mill. These testimonies show that enslaved people at the Freguesia Plantation had a similar agreement with their enslavers to cultivate their "private" crops. Moreover, the fact that these small crops aimed primarily to tie the enslaved to the plantation does not nullify its importance as a space conquered by the enslaved through bargaining, since the negotiation of plantation space by enslaved workers was also a physical manifestation of power relations on the plantation.

During a strike that happened on the Santana Plantation, in a treaty written by the enslaved people there outlining the conditions to return to the plantation, they demanded the right to cultivate their crops, showing the importance of this for enslaved people.[38] Bargaining for small improvements was one of the main ways enslaved people obtained some privileges. Usually, the enslavers agreed to some concessions to avoid the risk of retaliation from the enslaved side, showing that these small bargains were another important form of resistance acquired by the enslaved.

A MAROON COMMUNITY ACROSS THE BAY

Along with suicides and crimes, escapes were the main expression against the slavery system. In front of the Freguesia Plantation there was Maré Island (Figures 32 and 33), the third biggest island in the Bay of All Saints. Since Maré was only one mile from the Freguesia Plantation, many enslaved people tried to swim to the island. While many of them drowned during the crossing due to the dangerous waters of the bay, those who succeeded created hidden settlements on the northern part of the island. Today Maré has important quilombola communities formed by fishermen, shellfish collectors, and artisans. Most inhabitants of Bananeira, one of these communities located on the northeastern side of Maré Island, across from the Freguesia Plantation, are the descendants of the former enslaved of the plantation.[39]

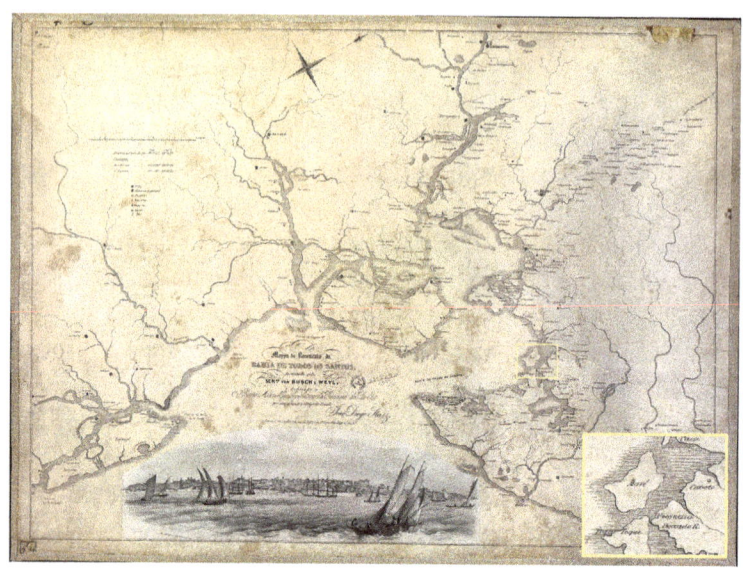

32 Map showing Maré Island

Maré Island, located one mile from the Freguesia Plantation. Enslaved people used to escape to the island to build settlements. Map of the Bay of All Saints by Von Busch and Weyl, 1836. Luso-Brazilian Library.

The lands around the Bay of All Saints' islands were/are generally formed by mangroves, which are a great source of seafood. Hence, after their escape, enslaved people were able to hide on the island and live from fishing and from the rich fauna that exists there. Runaway enslaved people adapted to the harsh conditions imposed by local nature and survived by obtaining food in natural forms. They also opened paths and built cabins covered by trees' leaves in the middle of the woods.[40] The quilombola communities at Maré Island still maintain the same survival techniques of their enslaved ancestry. It is very common to see them fishing and catching shellfish to sell in the markets of the neighboring areas.

The geographic isolation of Maré Island made it difficult for the capitães-do-mato to capture the fugitives, because they didn't know how many had managed to survive the crossing or whether they really crossed the bay instead of hiding in the forest on the plantation. Hence, it was safe for the fugitives to go to the island

33 View of Maré Island from the mill

From the ruins of the sugar mill, Maré Island can be seen in the distance, 2019. Photo by Doriane Meyer.

and build small settlements connected by narrow paths in the interior of the island's forest. According to the descendants of runaway enslaved people from the Freguesia Plantation, the enslaved men who crossed the bay to the island often went back in small canoes to retrieve their partners during the night.[41]

Chapter Conclusion

The use of surveillance and control over movement on plantations was a way for plantation owners to exert power and maintain control over their enslaved or other workers. Placing overseers' houses in strategic locations, close to senzalas, allowed plantation owners to keep a watchful eye on the workers and ensure that they were following rules and regulations. In the same way, the immense Big House helped reinforce the class hierarchy and maintain the plantation owner's position of power. Additionally, the owners tried to control enslaved people's movement through spaces on and between plantations to limit the interactions and mobility of their workers, which failed many times as the enslaved used the time walking around the neighborhood to strengthen friendships.

At the Freguesia Plantation, the Big House, the overseers' houses, and the senzalas were spatially adjacent. Enslaved people saw the enslaver's power every day through an imposing Big House architecture and the spatial organization characterized by control through the proximate physical presence of the slaveholder and the overseers. Simultaneously, while being subjected to panopticon surveillance, they also had the opportunity to observe the life on the plantation without being seen. Other times, they were all visible to each other. This was because the spaces where subjugated and subjugators coexisted on a daily basis were many times confined, since most of the other spaces of the plantation were covered by sugarcane fields and woods. The other option they had was to cross the bay and join the maroon community, which was not an option for everybody because of the high risk and because it meant leaving families and friends. Therefore, for most of the enslaved workers, the best form of appropriation of the spaces was in the form of bargains and unnoticed resistance.

In this way, the analysis of daily passive resistance helps in understanding the functioning of spaces acquired by the enslaved day after day, even if not explicitly. Therefore, the resistance of enslaved people assimilates a new dimension that starts not only from the presuppositions of enslaved autonomy but also from more concrete elements such as the conscious uses of plantation spaces, the networks of relationships developed by enslaved people beyond the plantation property, and the role of the enslaved in the production process.

The next chapter investigates a plantation with a singular spatiality. The Cajaíba Plantation was built on an island, where enslaved people had less mobility than those who lived on mainland plantations such as Freguesia.

Chapter Three

Cajaíba Sugarcane Plantation

. . . where life was nothing and sugar was all.

—W. E. B. DUBOIS, 1901[1]

Introduction

The epigraph suits the Cajaíba Plantation well, as it was infamous for the brutality of the Baron of Cajaíba and renowned for its magnificent architecture. The Institute of Artistic and Cultural Heritage of Bahia (IPAC-BA) has listed the Cajaíba Plantation's Big House and sugar mill as a national historic place since 2004.[2] The buildings were built around 1712–1715 on the island of Cajaíba near the city of São Francisco do Conde (Figure 34). The island can only be accessed by boat through the neighboring rivers or the Bay of All Saints. From a distance, one can see the imperial palm trees, the mansion, and the sugar mill. The buildings were elevated with a semicircular staircase that gives access to a front garden. The staircase is sometimes partially submerged when the Serigi River tide is high. The Big House and the sugar mill are two imposing buildings, erected side by side, with the Big House being farther away from the river, behind a garden. Although the extant buildings are not well preserved, many of them are in good shape. Therefore, it was possible to visit and analyze the environment, including the Big House, the sugar mill, and the overseer's house. The Cajaíba Plantation has different geography than most of the Recôncavo region plantations. Besides being on an island, it was on flat land, which was oftentimes favorable but at other times harmful for either the enslaver's surveillance or the resistance of the enslaved.

34 Cajaiba Plantation

Cajaíba Island, 2015. Photo by Carlos Santiago (@myphantomtoy).

The Region: São Francisco do Conde

The Indigenous communities who inhabited this region before the Portuguese arrived lived off of agriculture and fishing. They used paths in the forests and the river for navigation. Their communication with other communities was mainly through the rivers. Most of the locations still have Indigenous names such as Cajaíba, based on Cajá, which is a fruit very common on the island. Later, the Portuguese expelled the Indigenous peoples from their territories and appropriated the lands and paths in the exploration and occupation of the territories.

In 1618, a convent and a church were built on top of a hill from where, in 1697, the village of São Francisco do Conde would grow near the shore of the Serigi River (Figure 35).[3] In the past, the economic development and the wealth of the city was based on sugarcane plantations. Besides the production of sugar, the village had important fishing warehouses that were used to supply the capital and the neighboring cities with its products. After the abolition of slavery in 1888, the city experienced economic decline until 1947, when oil was discovered in the region. However, the municipal administration has not invested in its population even though it

35 Map highlighting São Francisco do Conde

The Bahian Recôncavo region. São Francisco do Conde microregion highlighted by the author. The red dot shows the location of the Cajaíba Plantation. IBGE/DGC, 2018.

receives significant oil taxes. Hence, the quilombola communities there, formed by the descendants of enslaved people, still survive on fishing and selling seafood.

Besides the mainland portion, the São Francisco do Conde region has four islands: Fontes, Paty, Bimbarras, and Cajaíba. The last two are private islands, and Cajaíba housed the plantation being studied in this chapter. The time frame of this study spans most of the eighteenth century, but the analysis also references the seventeenth and nineteenth centuries, when the plantation was in operation.

The seventeenth century was a phase of expansion for sugar commerce. However, as described before, it was also a period of crisis due to conflicts in the colony, high taxes, enslaved people's escapes, and the discovery of gold and diamonds in the southeastern part of the colony. Due to the last finding, a large number of enslaved people were moved to work in the mines. In addition, Dutch invasions, drought, and epidemics in the Recôncavo region were responsible for the disorganization and decrease in sugar production.[4] Moreover, the sugar economy also faced external competition from the French and Dutch plantations in the Caribbean due to the technological backwardness of the Brazilian sugar industry. Nevertheless, sugar commerce in Brazil recovered at the end of the seventeenth century, and it was still the most profitable product of the colony, even more than the gold and cotton that became important products in the eighteenth century due to the industrial revolution. During the eighteenth century, sugar commerce observed fluctuations in importance, price, and quantity. Another crisis marked the beginning of the century in sugar production due to the "colonial pact" between the European metropolis and their colonies, in which the colonies could only sell their products to their metropolis.[5] In 1763, Portugal moved the capital of the colony to Rio de Janeiro, which increased the crisis on the Recôncavo plantations as Salvador lost the position of being the main port of export.

In the early nineteenth century, helped by international crises such as the Haitian revolution, the Napoleonic Wars in Europe, and ensuing chaos in the Spanish colonies in America, Brazilian sugar commerce retook its place in international commerce.[6] Salvador and Rio de Janeiro were established as great ports and commerce centers at the end of the eighteenth century.[7] There were over 400 sugarcane plantations in the Recôncavo region. Portugal returned its attention to Salvador and the other cities of the Recôncavo, building many important government buildings. São Francisco do Conde received its first town hall and jail.

It was during this time that on the Cajaíba Plantation, Alexandre Gomes de Argolo Ferrão (1800–1870), later best known as the Baron of Cajaíba, was born.

History of the Cajaíba Plantation

The Cajaíba Plantation belonged to one of the oldest Bahian families. The Argolos arrived in Brazil with the first governor, Tomé de Souza, in 1549. Its first owner was the general governor of Brazil, Mem de Sá, during the sixteenth century. After his death, his daughter Filipa and her husband Fernando de Noronha, Count of Linhares, inherited his lands. However, the current buildings were constructed by José Joaquim de Argolo e Queiroz in the eighteenth century.[8] His son, Alexandre Gomes de Argolo Ferrão, the Baron of

Cajaíba, is recognized to this day as one of the cruelest slaveholders in Brazil. The stories about the Baron of Cajaíba were orally transmitted through generations, and the martyrdom of enslaved people on the Cajaíba Plantation represents an important part of the history of suffering and resistance for their descendants who still live in communities near Cajaíba Island. After the death of the baron, the plantation was transmitted to his homonymous son, Alexandre Gomes de Argolo Ferrão (1847–1878), best known as "the little baron," murdered by his enslaved workers. During the twentieth century, Bernardo Martins Catarino bought the island, and it later passed to his granddaughter Alice Maria R. dos Santos Marigliani. Today the island belongs to the city of São Francisco do Conde and is controlled by the secretary of tourism.

Spatial Organization

The buildings at the Cajaíba Plantation—Big House, sugar mill, senzalas, and overseer's house—formed a quadrilateral. The way they were distributed, and the material used in each building, reflected their hierarchical position on the plantation. The distribution was done in a way to control the workers and the production, and to show the economic and social differences between classes and ethnicities. The buildings were on the southeastern part of the island, a half mile from the city of São Francisco do Conde. The island, which is about five miles long and two miles wide, used to be covered by sugarcane fields, mangroves, and forests. According to archival documents, the only constructions were the Big House, the sugar mill, the overseer's house, and some reservoirs for fish farming. It is also known that they bred cattle on the island. Thus, it can be assumed that there were probably also stables as well as chicken coops and pigsties, which were very common on the farms at that time.[9]

Like most of the plantations in the Recôncavo region, although Cajaíba had vast lands, the buildings were close to each other. The front garden of the Big House and the sugar mill were on the shore of the river. Many plantations from the eighteenth century had their Big Houses close to the sugar mill so the enslaver could

36 Aerial View of Cajaíba Plantation

(1) Big House; (2) senzalas (enslaved people's quarters); (3) house of the overseer; (4) sugar mill. Square, numbers, and cardinal added by the author. Photo by Carlos Santiago (@myphantomtoy).

better control production. The overseer's house was on the side of the sugar mill and the senzalas. The four main buildings of the plantation formed a distribution similar to Vauthier's design (see chapter 1) and some plantations in the Caribbean, United States, and southeastern Brazil.[10] It was a common spatial distribution of control on flat lands (Figure 36).

Spaces of Power

Slavery is, by nature, a violent process, full of pain and suffering, with a legacy of racism, poverty, and social inequality. In the memories of some current residents of the city of São Francisco do Conde and neighboring quilombola communities, the Baron of Cajaíba is still referred to as a cruel man in his relationship with enslaved people, free workers, and enemies.[11] The plantation was planned in a way to maximize control over enslaved people.

37 Cajaíba Plantation Big House
The garden and the frontal staircase, 2019. Photo by Doriane Meyer.

BIG HOUSE

Although sugar commerce was in crisis during the eighteenth century, the architecture of Big Houses was splendid. The Cajaíba Plantation had a 1,100-square-meter (11,840-square-foot), two-floor neoclassical mansion, settled magnificently in the landscape, framed by imperial palm trees (Figure 37).

The preserved mansion has external marble stairs with iron railings, which give direct access to the second floor, where the family lived. In the center of the facade, the main door stands out, opening to rooms with richly decorated walls and ceilings. In the first hall, which was used as a vestibule, there was the Catholic altar for the private use of the family. The floor also had a dining room, a living room, six bedrooms, a kitchen, and a balcony toward the back of the house (Figure 38). Under the balcony, there was a storage area that opened to an enclosed backyard, which also gave access to domestic enslaved workers' rooms facing the back of the house. There

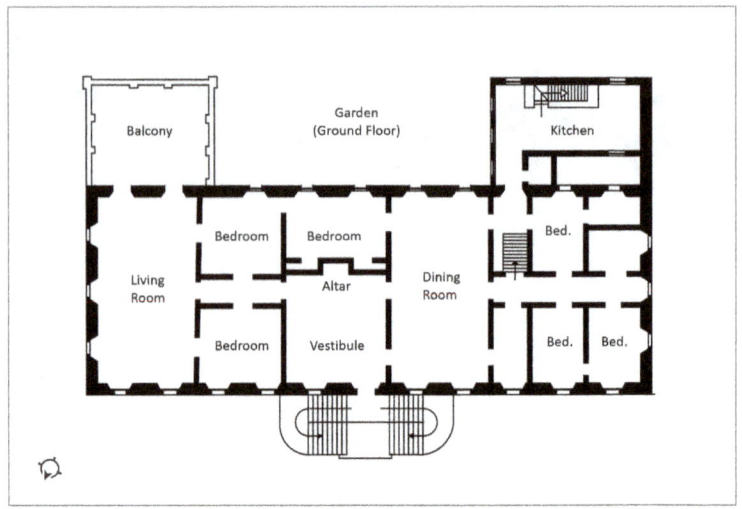

38 Plan of the second floor of Cajaíba's Big House

The floor where the family resided. Drawing by the author. Original plan courtesy of IPAC.

39 Front of the Big House

The external stairway of the Big House goes to the second floor where the family lived. Photo by Doriane Meyer, 2019.

40 Dining Room with the mirrors

The hanging mirrors, 1945. The baron used the mirrors to surveil outside during the meals. IPHAN Archives.

were two internal stairways to the ground floor; one linked to a secondary kitchen, and another linked to a small room probably where some of the enslaved domestic workers slept so they could be available during the night if the family needed something.

In front of the mansion, there was a garden with a passageway coated by Portuguese tiles. Toward the garden, the access to the storage area and administrative rooms was located on the first floor. The storage rooms were accessed by doors on the sides of the external stairs, and the administrative room was accessed by a central door under the stairs (Figure 39).

The Baron of Cajaíba controlled the plantation with extremely authoritarian power. His obsession to control could be seen in the dining room, from where he could watch outside through the mirrors strategically hung on the walls (Figure 40).

SUGAR MILL

The location and typology of the sugar mill were planned according to the type of workforce required for the milling machine and the enslaver's desired level of control over production. In the Recôncavo, animals or water power were typically used to mill the

41 Cajaíba Plantation Sugar Mill

Twelve arches decorate the frontal façade, 2019. Photo by Doriane Meyer.

cane, which depended on the topographical conditions and the existence of rivers near the plantations. Because the Cajaíba Plantation was on flat land, it was not possible to use water to generate energy for the milling machine; it used animal power, which was called trapiche.[12] The milling machines were probably rotated by oxen as there were cattle on the island. Besides milling the cane, the workers had to cook the sugar, purge (purify) it, separate it by quality, pack it, transport it to the docks, and load it onto ships. Usually, a plantation of the size of Cajaíba had about 200 workers between the enslaved and free people.

The sugar mill covered 942 square meters (10,140 square feet) in a trapezoidal shape. It was split into three long spaces with two rows of columns to support the roof of structural wood covered with ceramic tiles. The roof covered two parts of the mill, and the third part was open. Although there is no document showing how this mill worked in the past, according to some other similar mills, we can conclude that the milling machine was in the uncovered spaces, and the covered central space was used for cooking and purging the sugar. The space facing the river has twelve round

42 *View of the pier*

View of the pier in front of the sugar mill from a window of the Big House. From there, the enslaver could watch the sugar being loaded. IPHAN Archives.

arches and was probably the space to store the sugar before it was loaded onto boats (Figure 41). A pier in the front of the mill was used to load the sugar (Figure 42). It was in a position where the enslaver could watch the loading.

CHAPEL

The importance and influence of the Catholic Church were very clear during the times of slavery. Every plantation had a religious space, in a smaller or larger size, outside or inside the Big House. On the Cajaíba Plantation, there was only a small altar in the vestibule facing the main door of the house. Its location at the entrance of the first floor allowed people close to the family to attend in Mass without going to the private areas of the house (Figure 43). It is clear that the enslaved people did not attend Mass because the space was suited only for the family and a few more people. Also, knowing that the enslavers were very rigid with their enslaved workers, they probably did not like proximity to the enslaved.

43 Altar at the Vestibule Room

Family's private altar, 1945. Photo by Silvanísio Pinheiro. IPHAN Archives.

SENZALAS (ENSLAVED PEOPLE'S QUARTERS)

According to a local inhabitant of São Francisco do Conde,[13] the set of senzalas was behind the sugar mill. There are no photographs, plans, or documents showing its architecture or the number of enslaved people living there. It can be supposed that the senzalas

44 *The stairs to the enslaved people's rooms.*

Stairs to the rooms of domestic enslaved workers, 2019. Photo by Doriane Meyer.

were similar to the others from the same period—small rooms arranged in a row, attached to each other with only doors and a front
porch—toward the back of the Big House and the sugar mill.

On the ground floor of the mansion, there are rooms where
enslaved domestic workers used to sleep (Figure 44). These rooms

45 Window with Latticework

The window of the domestic enslaved people's quarters with iron latticework, 1945. Photo by Silvanísio Pinheiro. IPHAN Archives.

46 Overseer's house.

A simple construction, 2019. The decorative frames on the windows and door were added in 2016 for the filming of a soap opera. The house on the right side of the photo was also built later. Photo by Doriane Meyer.

were connected to the interior of the house and had iron lattice-work in the windows. These were probably for enslaved women who served the house during the night (Figure 45).

OVERSEER'S HOUSE

The house of the overseer followed the same austere construc-tion and typology seen on many other plantations of the Recôncavo (Figure 46). It had two rooms, probably one a living room and the other a bedroom. There is a bathroom annexed on the back, which was built later because the houses did not have bathrooms inside them in the eighteenth century.

From the house, the overseer could easily watch the sugar mill and the senzalas. His house was also toward the quad where enslaved people joined in the morning to receive the work instruc-tions. In 2016, a porch was added to the house during the recording of a soap opera on the island.

Forced labor and violence dictated the pace of life for enslaved people in the Recôncavo in the eighteenth century. Against this regime, enslaved people used various forms of resistance, such as escapes, dragging their feet to work, revolts, robberies, and suicide. On the Cajaíba Plantation, many enslaved people escaped to the northern part of the island and created small communities. These refuge places sometimes transformed into larger quilombola communities. To survive, fugitives hidden in these communities stole crops, weapons, and supplies, and recruited other enslaved people from nearby plantations. Often the fugitives gathered there would practice how to burn cane fields and steal weapons or animals. However, at the same time, they also created new ties and shared religions and cultures.

The island of Cajaíba has a significant historical and social meaning. If, for the official history of the Portuguese colonization it was important as a space for the production of sugar and control of enslaved workers, for the Afro-descendants, it was a Black space of revolts and other forms of resistance. As an act of resistance and the feeling that they have the right to the lands, many descendants of enslaved people from the Cajaíba Plantation ended up settling on the edge of the mangroves, where they sought their livelihood through fishing and shellfishing, still waiting to be compensated for what their ascendants built with suffering.

PHYSICAL AND PSYCHOLOGICAL RESISTANCE

While the baron (father) was alive, his daughter Miss Maria Augusta was in charge of the Cajaíba Plantation's activities in his absence. In one of her correspondences to her father, she wrote of the painful daily life of enslaved workers and showed concerns about how the overseer, called Lopes, treated them, "beating the slaves without mercy in their faces and chests."[14]

The Bahian Recôncavo, in general, and the Cajaíba Plantation, in particular, were notable for the cruelties of plantation owners. The enslavers and overseers severely punished enslaved workers who failed to follow orders. Some of them were tied to the pillory

47 The Tamarind Tree used as a pillory
The iron to secure the chains is still there, 2019. Photo by Doriane Meyer.

and whipped to death, some were thrown into furnaces or had their bodies mutilated. Histories of what used to happen on the Cajaíba Plantation were passed down from generation to generation, haunting the memories of the *quilombola* communities in this region of the Recôncavo.

Enslaved workers of the Cajaíba Plantation often reported to the police of São Francisco do Conde their desire to stop serving their enslavers. In February 1881, an enslaved woman called Clementina, who escaped from the Cajaíba Plantation with her daughter, denounced to the police the abuses she had suffered on the plantation.[15]

Even today, the Cajaíba Plantation shows traces of the baron's cruelty and the symbols of slavery—for example, a tree with hooks outside the Big House where enslaved workers were held to be whipped (Figure 47) and a well with spears (Figure 48) where enslaved people were thrown to die by drowning in the water from the river. These are only a few elements that survived the passage of time to show the psychological and physical torture enslaved

48 The well

The well inside the sugar mill where enslaved workers were thrown to drown, 2019. Photo by Doriane Meyer.

people suffered on that plantation. The Cajaíba Plantation became a symbol of resistance for the people that descended from the former enslaved people who lived there, showing that not only the habitus of subservience but also the endurance was transmitted through generations.

SIMULTANEOUS SURVEILLANCE

At dawn on September 3, 1878, several enslaved workers went inside the Big House and killed Alexandre Argolo, the "little baron" of Cajaíba,[16] who, like his father, was known for mistreating his enslaved workers with excessive work and sexual abuse. The violent stories narrated in judicial documents tell us a lot about the feelings and thoughts these workers had about their conditions and the motivations they had to plan their survival strategies. When enslaved people reached their limits, they revolted against the terrible treatment they had been suffering. Sometimes, they would impulsively kill the enslaver or overseer using a tool, or they could

49 View of the mill from the Big House

View of the back of the sugar mill from the Big House, 2019. This open space was probably used for the milling machine. Photo by Doriane Meyer.

plan it as they did with Alexandre Argolo. The baron and his son did not care about their enslaved workers, and they used and allowed many strategies to punish and coerce enslaved people. From the Big House of the Cajaíba Plantation, the enslavers could watch the outside environment, supervise the senzalas, the overseer's house, and the sugar production (Figure 49), and observe the physical punishment on the tree used as the pillory close to the Big House.[17]

Alexandre Gomes Ferrão de Argolo (the son), together with his sister, inherited the plantations that belonged to the Baron of Cajaíba eight years after the death of his father. Alexandre was responsible for the administration of the two most important plantations of the family—Cajaíba and Itatingui.[18] Following in the same steps as his father, who was recognized as one of the cruelest men of the slavery era, Alexandre did not care about enslaved workers. He also mistreated them.

For the above reason, some enslaved people from the Itatingui Plantation watched their enslaver's routine to plan for his murder.

50 View of the back of the Big House

A view of the back of the Big House from the senzalas (enslaved people's quarters), 1945. The windows of the domestic enslaved workers were also toward this backyard. IPHAN Archives.

This event shows that in the same way the enslaved were observed, they also observed the enslaver. Behind the slaveholders' and overseers' backs, they stole food, clothing, and money and did things that could result in financial loss for the enslaver. These were usually individual actions. When they acted in a group, the actions were more violent and generally planned, as shown by the murder of Alexandre Ferrão. The enslaved knew that the baron frequently abused enslaved women and went to sleep after the women left the Big House; hence, it was easy to kill him at that time. The enslaved workers who killed the baron wanted to show that their bodies did not belong to him and that the physical and psychological violence should stop. In the same way, enslaved people from the Cajaíba Plantation could observe the movements of the enslavers from their quarters (Figure 50) and from the sugar mill (Figure 51).

51 View from the Mill
A view of the Big House from the sugar mill, 2019. Photo by Doriane Meyer.

QUILOMBOLA COMMUNITIES—PAST AND PRESENT LINKED BY A
SYSTEMIC RACISM

Cajaíba Island is still mentioned as an area of conflict and resistance among the descendants of the formerly enslaved people from the plantation—who want the right to stay there—and the government authorities—who want them out.

Many descendants of the enslaved still live in the area where their ancestors formed quilombos. The acts of resistance of the past continue to be used as an example of the struggle of the quilombolas who are still constantly marginalized because they always remind society of their ancestors' past. The quilombos are the physical forms of resistance that Black people have maintained in the arduous effort to preserve their personal and historical identity.

During slavery, despite suffering many adversities, some quilombos near Cajaíba Island became strongly organized. They located themselves in transitional areas between the plantations and the forests. Places with hills were commonly used to create

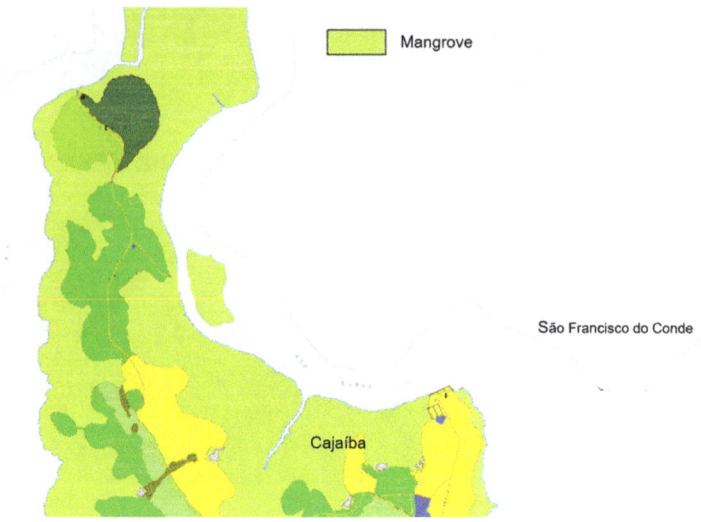

Mangrove

São Francisco do Conde

Cajaíba

52 *Map of Cajaíba Island*

Map of Cajaíba Island showing the mangrove areas. IPAC.

"autonomous" spaces because fugitives could easily see threats from these places. Although there was no hill at Cajaíba Island, the mangroves provided the right advantage during the escapes.

Having a plantation near a mangrove forest or a river was beneficial for a plantation because the transportation of products was cheaper and more profitable. However, this location was unfavorable for plantation owners when it came to enslaved people's escapes. The Cajaíba Plantation had a large extension of mangroves (Figure 52), with a rich ecosystem that helped runaway enslaved people in their escape. It was this environment that allowed enslaved workers to escape from the plantation to the northern side of the island where they could easily use the crops to hide from the enslaver's and overseer's sight and feed themselves with freshly caught crustaceans and seafood (Figure 53). The natural environment of the island and its topography suggest that enslaved people would have escaped through the middle of the island, where the cane fields were located, making it difficult to be seen from the Big House.

53 North Side of Cajaiba Island

The enslaved people used to escape to the northern part of the island in order to cross the river. In the distance, the author added an ellipse to show the location of the plantation's buildings. IPAC.

São Braz, located on the mainland, just across the northwestern part of Cajaíba Island (Figure 54), is one of the communities formed by descendants of formerly enslaved people from Cajaíba and other neighboring plantations. In this place, inhabitants have been developing practices of resistance since the slavery era. It produced and reproduced characteristic ways of life—surviving from the natural environment, keeping group union, fighting to maintain their culture and memories of their ancestry, among others—leading to the consolidation of their own territory when they formed the quilombo.[19]

However, the racial conflicts of slavery survived abolition, and after over 100 years, descendants of the enslaved people from the Cajaíba Plantation must still resist ethnic prejudices. The quilombola communities are still marginalized, showing that systemic racism is still strong in Brazilian society.

SUBSISTENCE FOODSTUFFS

One important element that appeared on plantations during the eighteenth century were fishponds, which included large artificial lakes linked to the ocean by a channel with floodgates to control

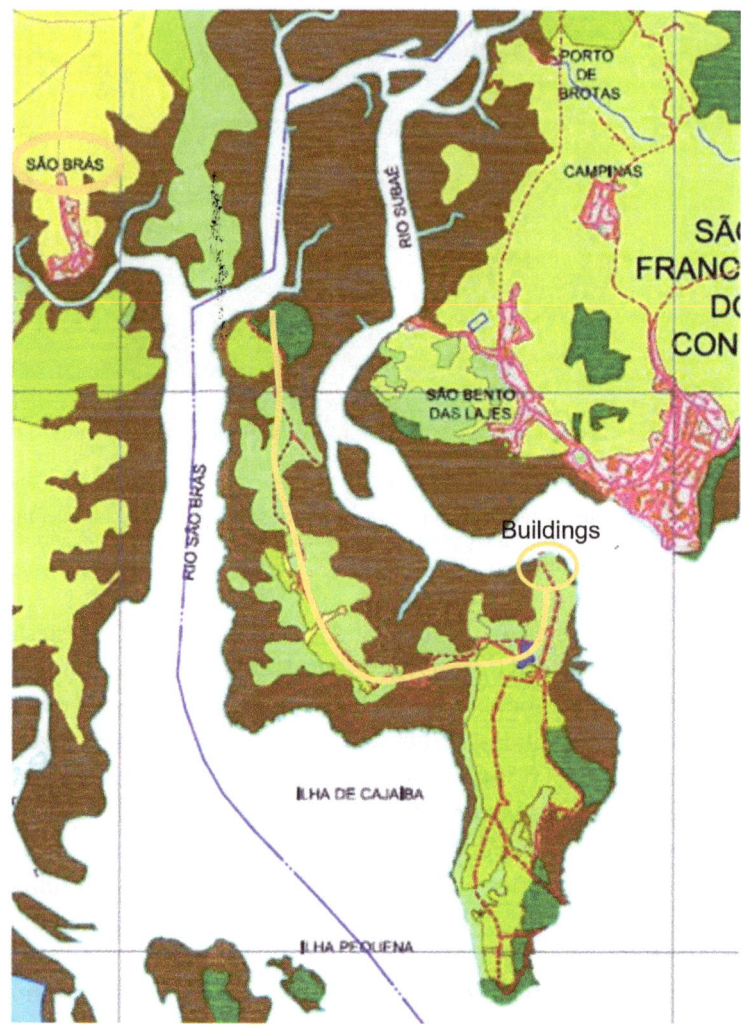

Buildings

54 Map of Cajaíba Island and São Bras

The brown areas are mangroves. The beige ellipse (added by the author) marks
the location of the buildings, and the beige line (added by the author) was
probably the route enslaved people used to flee, hiding in the forest until they
reached the northern part of the island. Later the São Bras community was built
across the river. IPAC.

55 Artificial Pond

A pond built for fishing, 2019. The gate showed in the picture used to slide to hold the fish inside the pond. Photo by Doriane Meyer.

water. The ponds provided food for the enslavers' families and the workers.[20]

At the Cajaíba Plantation there were two artificial ponds connected to the river. As Figure 55 shows, there was a vertical slide door to close it when they were full of water. Although it was an allowed activity, it was also a means of using the space of the plantation in a way that benefited enslaved workers. Fishing in these ponds was probably one important way for them to feel free.

Cajaíba Island was also rich in fruits and shellfish. Besides fish in the ponds, enslaved people used the spatiality of the island to find food and grow small crops. When Gabriel Sousa was visiting the Recôncavo region, he traveled on the Serigi River and described Cajaíba Island as a land with sugarcane fields and some small subsistence crops.[21] The island had different sources of foodstuffs. They found different kinds of shellfish and crustaceans in the mangroves; they fished in the rivers around the island; they cultivated different species of fruits; and they had small crops of vegetables, beans, cassava, and some other roots.[22]

The domestic farming of chickens and pigs was also common in the region. Enslaved people also raised animals and shared the production, such as milk and meat, with the enslaver.[23] Some enslaved people were also allowed to go to the city of São Francisco do Conde to sell their produce, where they also had opportunities to build relationships and obtain crucial information to help them if they wanted to escape from the island. It is known that the baron accused some enslaved people of hiding money, and when he had this suspicion, whether it was true or not, he would throw the worker to drown into the well located in the sugar mill.

Because the enslavers and overseers at the Cajaíba Plantation were cruel, it is possible that most of the food enslaved people ate was cultivated/raised by them. This meant more work in their spare time, but it also meant freedom to cultivate and to have a feeling that the spaces of the island also belonged to them.

Chapter Conclusion

Because Cajaíba was located on an island, unlike most plantations, the geography restricted the actions of enslaved people. Therefore, except when they fled across the river, the appropriation of spaces took place more like a set of actions within the limits of the island. During their "rest" time, the enslaved fished, raised animals, and cultivated small crops for their subsistence.

The Cajaíba Plantation has a history of excessive punishment and suffering for the enslaved people who lived there. Hence, quilombola communities formed by descendants of runaway enslaved people from the Cajaíba Plantation share with the island a feeling of belonging in terms of social identity and ancestry. The presence of punishment tools from the past is viewed by descendants of enslaved people as a powerful reminder of the resilience that their ancestors maintained against a system that sought to crush their spirits. The punishments they suffered due to acts of rebellion, escape attempts, or even small forms of resistance, such as the preservation of cultural traditions and practices, were a means for enslaved individuals to assert their humanity and resist the dehumanizing effects of slavery. Their ancestors' struggles against the slavery system allow the individuals of today's communities to understand the social context in which they are inserted, which is still full of prejudice against Black people.

Therefore, the island is a symbol of resistance of the enslaved people that lived, fought, and/or died at the Cajaíba Plantation. As João Reis points out, "It is obvious that slaves and quilombolas were forced to change things they would not change if they were not subjected to slavery and colonial pressure, but it was their direction that led to many of these changes, as they did not allow them to become what the masters wanted."[24]

The next chapter will show a plantation that, despite having clear panoptic surveillance, had a quilombo built within its lands without being discovered. In addition, the enslaved people of the Vitória Plantation have a history of a strong transmission of African culture through religion, food, and music.

Chapter Four

Vitória Sugarcane Plantation

Slaves sing most when they are most unhappy. The songs of the slave represent the sorrows of his heart; and he is relieved by them, only as an aching heart is relieved by its tears.

—FREDERICK DOUGLASS[1]

Introduction

During the slavery era, the music played, chanted in African dialects, and the religion practiced in parallel to Catholicism were used as forms of resistance by enslaved people from the Vitória Plantation to transmit African cultures through generations.

The Nossa Senhora da Vitória Plantation (Figure 56), bought by Pedro Rodrigues Bandeira in 1812, became one of the most prominent plantations in the region, at one time housing 250 enslaved people and producing 142 tons of sugar a year.[2] The plantation, which is located in the Cachoeira region, was built when the sugar economy returned the growth on the region.

In spite of the fact that there are only ruins of the buildings and access to the plantation site is not easy, the Vitória Plantation is still one of the most visited in the Recôncavo region. The region and the plantation site attract not only researchers from many areas, but also seduce tourists through the imposing Big House on the shore of the Paraguaçu River.

The Region: The City of Cachoeira and the Paraguaçu River

The Cachoeira region (Figure 57) is linked to the colonization process of the Bahian Recôncavo. In 1531, after the expedition of

56 Vitoria Plantation

On the shore of the Paraguaçu river, 1939. Photo by Eric Hess. IPHAN Archives.

European explorers Martim Afonso de Souza and Paulo Dias Adorno, in which they traveled the region along the Paraguaçu River, a process of local settlement started in the region. Driven by the need for a sugar economy, the Portuguese initially enslaved the Amerindians who already lived in the region. However, after they were mostly exterminated by fighting and disease, the Portuguese turned to enslaved Africans—which was noted in an earlier chapter.

The first plantation in the region belonged to the Genoese Paulo Dias Adorno, around which the village of Cachoeira started to grow following its official founding in 1693.[3] By the end of the sixteenth century, the Cachoeira region had five plantations. The village of Cachoeira was settled at the navigable limit of the Paraguaçu River, on the border between two economically complementary regions: the Recôncavo and the hinterland.[4] During the eighteenth century, Cachoeira underwent a development boom due to the high price of sugar and abundance of gold found in the hinterland, with the town serving as an entrepôt for a vast inland region. As the region's sugar

57 Map highlighting Cachoeira

The Recôncavo and its regions. Cachoeira region highlighted by the author. The red dot shows the location of the Vitória Plantation. IBGE/DGC, 2018.

commerce grew, it created a necessity for supporting infrastructure, which allowed the village to grow quickly and officially become a city in 1837. The Vitória Plantation's buildings were built soon after the village started to develop into a city.

The events that led to the success of the Vitória Plantation started at the end of the eighteenth century. After the industrial revolution, cotton, coffee, and sugar went from being luxury products to mass consumer products in England. Thereby, despite the thriving sugar economy of Cuba, the necessity for more workers in the Recôncavo increased to meet the demands of a growing external market. This intensified the slave trade in the region. Dale Tomich calls this new mass human importation, the "second slavery."[5] According to Tomich, the Atlantic traffic of the nineteenth century was not a mere continuity of the previous centuries. In the 1800s, they took on different characteristics, with sugar, coffee, and cotton in command of the slave traffic chain of Cuba–Brazil–United States. It constituted an enormous paradox because England banned the traffic in 1807, but England continued nourishing the slavery of these three locations with its increasing demand for sugar, coffee, and cotton. Linked to modern capitalism, the nineteenth-century slave trade was reconfigured in an even more potent way under the British hegemony. These global trade dynamics of the nineteenth century stimulated the expansion of the Vitória Plantation's sugar production, to which we turn next.

History of the Vitória Plantation

The Vitória Plantation appeared in the historical and socioeconomic context of the Recôncavo region between the late eighteenth century and the beginning of the nineteenth century. In 1812, Brazilian Commander Pedro Rodrigues Bandeira (1767–1835), son of a Portuguese merchant,[6] bought the plantation. Bandeira, a rich businessman who also owned two other neighboring plantations—Buraco and Conceição[7]—donated a lot of money to churches and a variety of other institutions, which gave him vast power. A proprietor of great fortune, he was one of the wealthiest men in Brazil in the nineteenth century. In 1818, Bandeira invested in shipyards for the establishment of steam navigation, which made the transport of sugar from the Recôncavo plantations to the port of Salvador faster before being exported to Europe. Bandeira also owned several ships that were linked to the Atlantic slave trade and to the navigation trade between the main cities of Europe and Asia. Additionally, Bandeira was linked to the most prominent politicians of Bahia, which caused him to support Brazil's independence from Portugal in 1822.[8]

Bandeira never married and probably lived with his sister Maria, who, according to the 1835 census, lived on the Buraco Plantation near the Vitória Plantation.[9] In 1835, there were about a thousand people living on his three plantations, including enslaved and free workers.[10] Bandeira passed away on October 14, 1835,[11] leaving his plantations to his niece Tereza Clara do Nascimento Viana and her three children, Francisco, Egas, and Pedro Barreto de Aragão. Tereza Clara was married to Salvador Muniz Barreto de Aragão (1789–1865), known as the first Baron of Paraguaçu.[12] After their deaths, the plantation was assumed by their son, a German-educated attorney, Egas Muniz Aragão, who moved to live there with his German wife. They had four children, and the family lived on the Vitória Plantation longer than any other. His brother, Francisco Muniz

Barreto de Aragão (1813–1901), the second Baron of Paraguaçu, was born in Salvador and died in Hamburg, Germany, where he was the consul general of Brazil. In 1858, Robert Ave-Lallemant, a colleague of the consul Francisco in Germany, mentioned in his travel book that he visited the Vitória Plantation and was impressed with the hospitality of the family, mainly by the culture of Egas Aragão's wife and the education of the children, who spoke French and German and had a private tutor living in the house.[13]

In 1936, engineer Francisco Muniz Barreto de Aragão, son of the second Baron of Paraguaçu, assumed ownership of the plantation and expanded the third floor of Vitória's Big House. The last sugar production was in 1950, and after Francisco Aragão's death, the family abandoned the plantation.[14] Aragão's heirs gave away part of the lands to the workers who were living there for decades and who were the descendants of the enslaved people who worked at the Vitória Plantation.[15] In 1954, the IAA (Sugar and Alcohol Institute) bought the plantation and gave it to Bahia's government in 1969. Since December 13, 1973, the navy has used the unoccupied parts of the property. The former plantation can now be reached by canoe or by a road that connects it to the city of Cachoeira.

Since March 23, 1943, the National Historical and Artistic Heritage Institute (IPHAN) has listed the plantation as a national historic place.[16] In 1983, the extant buildings were refurbished by the PróMemória National Foundation under the responsibility of the National Historical and Artistic Heritage Secretary (SPHAN). In my visit in 2019, the house was used by poor fishermen. With the walls and roof partially destroyed, the Big House is in deplorable condition, and the other buildings on the plantation have completely disappeared. The doors of the Big House were stolen, and all the windows were broken. Nevertheless, even in ruins, the impressive Big House still calls attention of those who pass by on the river (Figure 58).

As previously mentioned, most buildings on plantations in the Recôncavo region have disappeared over time; a few have one building remaining, usually in ruins, while only some, such as Freguesia and Cajaíba plantations, still have their main structures intact. Despite the fact that the buildings on Vitória Plantation were more

58 *Vitória Plantation Big House*

The manor stands out in the landscape, 2017. Photo by Paul R. Burley, CCBY-SA 4.0. Wikimedia Commons.

recent than those on the other two plantations, as shown in Figure 58, only the Big House survived, albeit in ruins. However, there is a rich documentation about Vitória in the archives—plans, photographs, paintings—and books written by foreign travelers. Therefore, to better analyze the spatial organization of the buildings at the Vitória Plantation, I reproduced a three-dimensional model of the plantation based on archival materials and site analyses.

Spatial Organization

The Vitória Plantation covered an area of 1,300 hectares (3,212 acres) and reached 97 meters (318 feet) at its highest topographical point. Built three miles from the city of Cachoeira, the plantation was next to three other plantations: Conceição, to the north; Buraco, to the south; and Embiara, to the east.

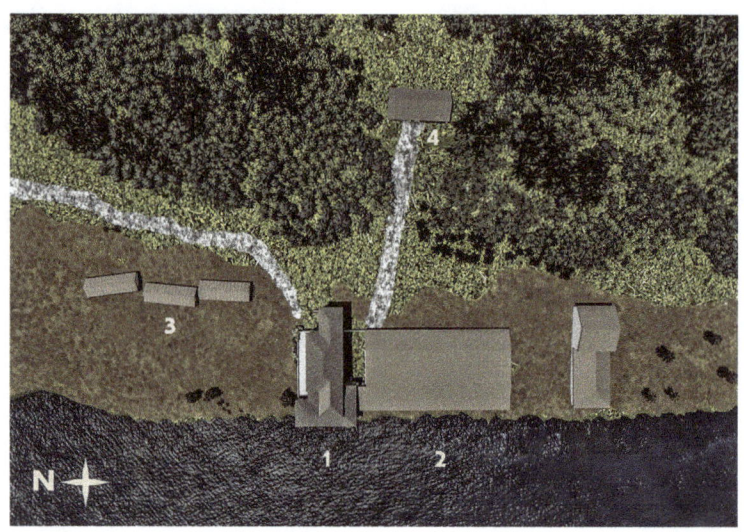

59 Vitoria Plantation Spatial Organization

Digital model of the Vitória Plantation. (1) Big House; (2) sugar mill; (3) senzalas (enslaved people's quarters); (4) overseer's house. Three-dimensional model designed by Doriane Meyer according to archival documents, paintings, and photographs.

In the nineteenth century, the Vitória Plantation had a few buildings, the sugarcane field, small subsistence crops, and a vast natural reserve of the Atlantic Forest. The small crops and the space for animals—oxen, horses, donkeys, and pigs—were located on the south side of the built space. The sugarcane fields were on the north side. The chicken coop was in the back of the senzalas. The east side of the plantation was occupied by a dense forest on a hill, and to the west was the Paraguaçu River (Figure 59).

The Big House and the mill were the two most expensive and prominent buildings at the Vitória Plantation. They were built of stones and tiles, contrasting with the clay-and-straw houses of the enslaved people. The durable material of the house gave it a character of temporal continuity, serving to legitimize and reproduce hierarchical social relationships through time. The location of the mill next to the river allowed it to have a small port and to draw a constant water supply through the aqueduct.

60 Three-dimensional Model of Vitória Plantation

From the Big House, the enslaver had a view of the production, the senzalas, and the river. Digital model designed by Doriane Meyer according to archival documents, paintings, and photographs.

As already observed, although plantations in the Recôncavo had vast areas, their buildings were usually close to each other. On Vitória, the Big House was attached to the mill, forming a unitary layout; the senzalas sat near the Big House to keep the enslaved people under the enslaver's eye; and the overseers' house was perched up on a hill, behind the mill, probably to keep the center of production under control and have a panopticon view of the plantation (Figure 60).

Spaces of Power

When planning the location of the buildings on a plantation, besides thinking about the absolute control over enslaved workers, location was important in the social and spatial structure, especially the relation of the Big House to other activity areas and buildings such as chapels and senzalas. The Vitória Plantation's Big House took a significant hierarchical position for those who lived and worked there and for its visitors. Occupying a commanding position, the central point of the Big House enabled and demonstrated constant surveillance by the enslaver. This strategy of domination had the purpose of reproducing social hierarchy.

The Big House of the Vitória Plantation was initially built with two complete floors. During the nineteenth century, the heirs of Pedro Bandeira renovated the house and included the third floor. The building has simplistic forms with some neoclassical decoration. The austerity was a characteristic of Big Houses from the nineteenth century.[17] Vitória's Big House, like any large residence from its period, was divided into private, social, and service spaces. A covered walkway, which also served as access to the mill, divides the ground floor into two parts. Facing the river was the administrative area. On the other side was the chapel, a salon with marble floors, guest rooms, a storage area, and bedrooms for the domestic enslaved workers. The unfamiliar guests were accommodated in bedrooms on the first floor with doors to the outside of the house, toward the senzalas.[18] Domestic enslaved workers slept in the bedrooms on the opposite side, toward the sugar mill, with doors open to a service yard used for domestic chores. On the second floor, the living room and the verandas provide expansive views of the exterior. The private parts of the house—the family bedrooms, dining room, and service areas—were kept mostly hidden. An internal stairway connected the two private areas on the second and third floors (Figure 61). Besides the family, only domestic enslaved workers could circulate in the private areas. Other enslaved people were never allowed in these areas without previous authorization. The intimate portion of the house was usually the mistress's domain, where she controlled the enslaved women.[19] From the second-floor windows, the mistress could observe and supervise all the movements in the service yard, controlling the tasks either by intervening personally or simply by observing the entire household production process.

Besides being the spaces where guests were usually welcomed, the verandas of the house were spaces for the surveillance and control of outside activities. From the windows in the three main facades of the Vitória Plantation's Big House, it was possible to see

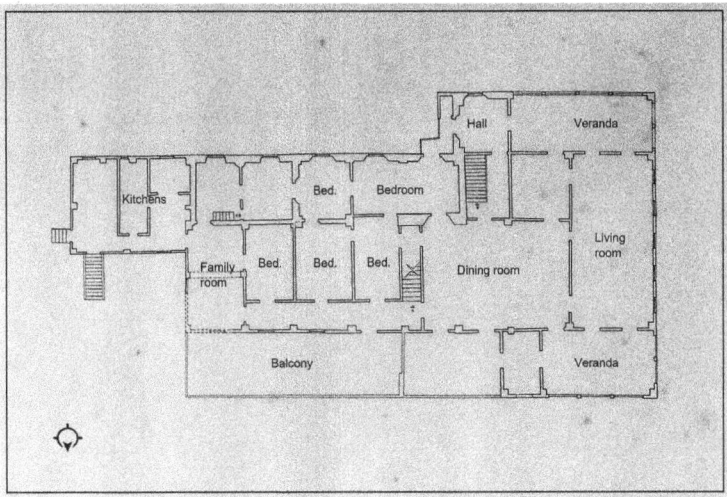

61 Plan of the second floor of Vitória's Big House

The floor where the family resided had the living room and the verandas facing towards the river. Room tags added by author. IPHAN Archives.

all the vessels traversing the river. The house was built imposingly near the sugar mill, slightly advancing into the river to be more highlighted, and could be seen from a distance, which symbolically marked the proprietor's superior status.

SUGAR MILL

The production unit was built in a flat area on the shore of the Paraguaçu River, in front of which was a small wharf for boats to take sugar to the port of Salvador for export. Access to water represented a vital resource for the plantation. The ruins and an archival photograph indicate that an aqueduct was linked to the center of the mill, which provided fresh water to the plantation, generating energy for the milling machine (Figures 62 and 63). Water-powered mills (Figure 64) increased productivity, sometimes doubling that of animal-powered mills. Other sources of energy were also used on other plantations, such as humans or steam. The former was used in sugar mills of other regions, and the latter was used after the modernization of sugar production in the late nineteenth century.

62 Ruins of the Aqueduct

The ruins of the aqueduct, which used to transport water to the sugar mill, are now covered by bushes, 2018. Photo by Doriane Meyer.

63 Aqueduct of Vitória Plantation

A view of the aqueduct and the back of the sugar mill, showing the place where cane was stored before being milled, 1939. Photo by Eric Hess. IPHAN Archives.

64 Milling machine

An example of a sugar mill with a similar structure to the one at the Vitória Plantation. Painting by Frans Post, 1640. Royal Museum of Fine Arts in Brussels.

The sugar mill formed a unitary layout with the Big House. This innovation, common in the nineteenth century, aimed to better control production and labor.[20] Like the Big House, the sugar mill was a simple brick construction with spaces to store the cane, the milling machine, the ovens to cook sugar, and the areas for purging it, separating it by quality, and boxing it. On the south side of the sugar mill, there were some buildings and a two-floor small house. They were probably used for storage, carpentry, and a sickroom. The second floor of the small house was probably occupied by drivers or by enslaved workers with special functions such as sugar masters, carpenters, and locksmiths (Figure 65).

CHAPEL

At the Vitória Plantation, it is still possible to find traces of Our Lady of Victory Chapel, located inside the house, near the main entrance (Figure 66). The use of imported and expensive decorated tiles in these rooms highlights their importance in the religion and the economy of the plantation. The churches also had an important social role, creating a space of correlation between the enslaver and his enslaved workers. At the same time, they were also segregated spaces where enslaved people, who, although they had permission to watch Mass, had to watch it separated from the enslaver's family

65 Small Buildings at Vitoria Plantation

On the south side of the Vitória Plantation (right on the photo), there were small buildings used for storage, carpentry, a sickroom, and housing for workers with special functions. Photo by Arthur Wischral. APEB.

66 Our Lady of Victory Chapel

The interior of Vitória's Chapel, 1939. The main door was located behind the benches, and on the left side were the doors that opened toward the senzalas (enslaved people's quarters). Photo by Eric Hess. IPHAN Archives.

67 Outside doors of Our Lady of Victory Chapel

North facade of the Big House showing the outside doors of the chapel on the
left, 1939. Photo by Eric Hess. IPHAN Archives.

and guests, highlighting the social hierarchy. For instance, in the
chapel of the Vitória Plantation, the enslaved people did not sit with
the enslaver's family. Instead, the lateral doors were kept open for
them to watch Mass from outside (Figure 67).

In addition to the chapel, there was also a small altar in one
of the columns of the sugar mill (Figure 68), which probably was
there in the hope of protecting the production, or perhaps to show
enslaved workers that they were also observed by "God."

SENZALAS (ENSLAVED PEOPLE'S QUARTERS)

The senzalas were located on the bottom of the hill. The Big House
forms two sides of a quad with the senzalas, which made them constantly visible. Different from the Big House and the mill, the senzalas were built of wattle and daub (pau-a-pique or taipa-de-mão,
in Portuguese), which was interlaced bamboo walls covered with
mud. The roofs were initially made of straw and later assembled of
wood with clay tiles (Figure 69). The senzalas had doors, windows,
and a porch facing the quad. According to archival photographs,

68 The Little Altar in the column of the sugar mill

The presence of the altar may have served as divine protection for the production, 2018. Photo by Doriane Meyer.

69 Senzalas at Vitoria Plantation

One row of senzalas at the Vitória Plantation, 1939. On the right side there is a fence with a chicken coop in the background. Photo by Eric Hess. IPHAN Archives.

there were three rows with twelve senzalas shared by around 240 enslaved people.[21] The enslaved people who lived in the senzalas were the ones who worked in the field and in the sugar mill. According to quilombola Detinho, a resident in the lands that belonged to the Buraco Plantation, the senzalas were overcrowded.[22] Because of the enormous number of enslaved people, another option is that there were more senzalas close to the cane field. However, this hypothesis is difficult to either prove or disprove as there is hardly any evidence about other senzalas at the Vitória Plantation; therefore, except for the domestic enslaved workers who slept on the first floor of the Big House, the rest shared the senzalas.

During his visit, Avé-Lallemant expressed indignation when he saw the senzalas of the Vitória Plantation. He described them as similar to dark stables full of enslaved people living together in small spaces.[23] In contrast, during their visit, Candler and Burges found that at the Vitória Plantation enslaved workers were treated with "decent clothing," "abundant food," and with the "same toil of the free workers." They also had permission to marry, have their own crops, leave their "property" to whom they wanted, and save money to buy their manumissions. Nevertheless, as they also observed, if there was anything wrong, it would be hidden from them. In addition, they observed that the enslaved always had a melancholic expression on their faces.[24]

OVERSEERS' HOUSE

The houses of the overseers, like the senzalas, were also a simple construction. They were made of wattle and daub, and they were covered by clay tiles. The Vitória Plantation probably had two overseers in command of the plantation and supervision of enslaved people and some drivers, who were under their command.

The overseers' house was the only building on the Vitória Plantation built on the hill, from where they could see the other buildings of the plantation, suggesting a vigilant position (Figure 70). In fact, it was rather common for planters to build the houses of overseers in places with a privileged view of the productive spaces and the circulation routes of enslaved workers.[25] Overseers were responsible for the day-to-day working of the plantation and were given surveillance capacity comparable to that of the owner, although their presence was less psychological and spiritual and more tangible, often in the cruelest of ways. Although there is no direct evidence of whether the Vitória Plantation had, like many other Brazilian plantations, a pillory, or any other device for torture, it is certain that physical punishment was used on this plantation. It had abuse and torment, as well as violent resistance on the part of the enslaved. At one point the enslaved workers of the Vitória Plantation killed the overseer and his brother.

Almost everything on a plantation was controlled by the overseers because "absentee landlordism" was very common.[26] There were multiple cases of abuse on plantations during the absence of the owners, including physical, verbal, and sexual. In the case of the murder of the overseer and his brother mentioned above, this was likely the case because Pedro Bandeira was a very busy businessman and used to spend a lot of time traveling.

70 Three-dimensional model showing the overseer's house

Vitória Plantation landscape showing the overseer's house on the hill. Digital model designed by Doriane Meyer according to archival documents, paintings, and photographs.

Spaces of Resistance

Enslavers and/or overseers used the built environment to install power from every direction, dominating the enslaved physically and psychologically. Enslaved people were subordinate to the power of the wealthy owner, the distant sight of the overseer, and the nearby presence of the drivers. This built environment took advantage of the topography and other geographic features, distributing main buildings in such a way as to control the most important and valuable resource at hand: the enslaved bodies of men, women, and children. However, enslaved people always found ways to resist this oppression.

SIMULTANEOUS SURVEILLANCE

On the night of March 22, 1827, about forty enslaved workers from Vitória went to the overseer's house and killed both the overseer and his brother.[27] It shows that simultaneous surveillance is one of the elements commonly used by all the enslaved who wanted to contravene the slavery system.

The layout of the Vitória Plantation highlighted a hierarchical arrangement. It imposed order and visual control over the space.

71 View of the senzalas from the Big House

Views of the senzalas and cane fields from the Big House. Three-dimensional model designed by Doriane Meyer according to archival documents, paintings, and photographs.

Besides closely watching the production of sugar, the enslaver could also see both sides of the terrain from the enormous windows of the Big House. The social life of enslaved people occurred in front of their dwellings, so their festivities were also watched from the Big House (Figure 71). As anthropologist Adam Smith and archaeologist Nicholas David point out, there are two major forms of spatial domination: appropriation and exclusion.[28] It is noted that on the Vitória Plantation, they used both forms to control enslaved people's spatiality. When the enslaved workers' quarters were built near the Big House, the enslaver was using proximity as a strategy of power. He was appropriating enslaved people's social spaces, even keeping them under surveillance during their leisure.

The other form, exclusion, was done in many ways, such as control over circulation. For instance, enslaved people needed permission to leave plantations and had their time outside closely monitored. Another example of exclusion happened during the Sunday Masses. As previously mentioned, Nossa Senhora da Vitória Chapel had lateral doors that were kept open to allow enslaved workers to watch Mass, as they were forbidden inside the chapel.

72 Lateral doors of the Chapel

North facade of the Big House showing the lateral doors of the chapel and the stairs to the Big House's service zone. Three-dimensional model designed by Doriane Meyer according to archival documents, paintings, and photographs.

The house also had stairs in the back linking the outside to the service area. These stairs were the limit for nondomestic enslaved workers when they needed to deliver something to the house, as only the domestic enslaved could circulate in the private areas of the Big House. (Figure 72). As Dell Upton points out, the separation of social space can be interpreted as an expression of power.[29] The spatial division of class also marked the separation of races, showing that even in a congregational religious event, the Black population remained marginalized.

The view of the overseer from his house on top of the hill demonstrates that he could observe most of the social and productive spaces of the plantation without being seen (Figure 73). To help them in the surveillance, there were also drivers who had even more intimate interaction with and control over enslaved workers than the overseers, as they were responsible for constant supervision of the cane field and the mill production.

Nonetheless, as they were being observed, enslaved workers were also observing. From their quarters, the mill, and the cane fields, they could monitor the oppressors' movements and use this in their favor (Figures 74 and 75). By watching their movements, they could articulate small acts of resistance, escapes, and even crimes.

73 View from the house of the overseer

From his porch, the overseer could observe the activities taking place on the plantation. Three-dimensional model designed by Doriane Meyer.

74 View from the senzalas

View of the overseer's house and Big House from the senzalas' patio. Three-dimensional model designed by Doriane Meyer according to archival documents, paintings, and photographs.

When the enslaved killed the overseers, it was not the beginning of a revolt, as the enslaved were quiet inside the senzalas when the police arrived. Hence, this act, probably a reaction against the abuse of violence, shows that the vigilance imposed over enslaved workers was not always efficient.

75 View from the sugar mill

View of the overseer's house from the sugar mill. Three-dimensional model designed by Doriane Meyer according to archival documents, paintings, and photographs.

"TABULEIRO DA VITÓRIA"—A MAROON SETTLEMENT INSIDE THE FOREST

As a consequence of the constant control and violence, many revolts happened in the Recôncavo region, most of the time commanded by African-born enslaved workers. In 1825, the Vitória Plantation had 217 enslaved people (137 male Afro-Brazilian, 48 female Afro-Brazilian, and 32 African female). Among them, there were no African men; all the men enslaved on the Vitória Plantation were born in Brazil. According to Reis, Bandeira's preference for Brazilian-born enslaved workers suggests a desire to prevent rebellions, as Africans were responsible for some of the most devastating events that caused plantations to burn and production to be destroyed.[30] Enslaved Afro-Brazilians, called criollos, were more peaceful because they had never known freedom. Their acts of resistance were primarily limited to bargaining with the enslavers, pretending they were sick, and running away for several days. Hence, the local authorities were never notified of any big revolution at the Vitória Plantation.

The enslaved people at the Vitória Plantation could execute most of their practices in agreement with the hierarchical system imposed by the enslavers; however, they also took advantage of the available circumstances to subvert this space, using it according to their practices and representations. As they were more prone to peaceful resistance rather than setting a field on fire or destroying the production, many of them preferred to run away for short periods or forever. The topographical environment of the Vitória Plantation, a mountainous area with a dense forest, provided good conditions for the creation of quilombos on the top of the hill, near the course of the rivers, where they could cultivate small crops for their subsistence. Paths and trails inside the forest were crucial elements that helped them secretly escape to gather on the hill, as it was hard for the capitães-do-mato to reach them there. Enslaved people could escape without returning or just take breaks during the night, returning in time for the morning tasks without having their absence noted by the overseers. Through the process of their escape, enslaved people expressed control over the spatiality of movement. When they used the forest in their favor, they demonstrated control over a part of the plantation space. Inside the forest, enslaved workers from Vitória articulated control over spatiality and could meet with enslaved people from the neighboring plantations, strengthen their net of friendships, practice their religions, exchange their cultures, create art forms, and develop family identities. These communities did not aim to demolish the system, as most of them only wanted to live well near plantations borders.[31] Therefore, the occupation of the areas belonging to the plantation constituted both appropriation of spaces and a challenge to the command imposed over them.

Today, these old quilombos are certified communities recognized as historical places.[32] They are called Tabuleiro da Vitória (Figure 76) and Tabuleiro do Buraco, which are formed by a hundred families, descendants of enslaved people who escaped from the Vitória Plantation and the neighboring Buraco Plantation. In the beginning, the collectivity of sharing the same space and the same historical heritage unified the community.[33] Later, after the abolition of slavery, some of the former enslaved people living in the settlement went back to work on the plantation in exchange for a wage. In the twentieth century, after the activities definitively

76 Tabuleiro da Vitoria

Tabuleiro da Vitória is the highest point of the Vitória Plantation. It marked the limits among Vitória, Buraco, Imbiara, and Guaibinha plantations. Map data: Google Earth, Maxar Technologies CNES/Airbus, 07/16/18.

finished at the Vitória Plantation, the heirs donated the lands on top of the hill to the residents of the communities, whose descendants are still living there to this day. These communities share the same social, cultural, and economic situation and coexist as if they belong to the same family. Claiming everybody as relatives, sociocultural relations marked these settlements as having a common beginning—a time when their ancestors were enslaved on the same plantations. It shows that the sense of kinship and spatial belonging was kept and passed through generations. The permanence of the descendants of former enslaved people in these traditional territories shows its historical and cultural strength of resistance to the dominant land system.

ENSLAVED PEOPLE'S CROPS AND THE JOINING NEIGHBORHOOD

Several travelers testified that the enslaved of the Vitória Plantation could have their own subsistence crops, which they could use for themselves or sell in the city at the Sunday market. While this showed a kind of agency exercised by enslaved people, at the same time, it was also a form of control. In the enslavers' vision, this was one method of holding enslaved people on the plantation and preventing their escape. However, from the enslaved perspective, this

77 The Road to Cachoeira

The arrows (added by the author) show the road from the Vitória Plantation to the city of Cachoeira. The road passed inside Conceição Plantation.

Map data: Google Earth, Maxar Technologies CNES/Airbus, 07/16/18.

shows that many were authorized to leave the plantation and have a way to make a little profit and form friendships.[34]

Between the Vitória Plantation and the city of Cachoeira, there was the Conceição Plantation, which also belonged to Pedro Bandeira's family, separated from the Vitória Plantation by only fences and gates. During their visit to Vitória, Candler and Burgess recalled that they went on a trip to the city on horseback, passing by pastures and cane fields. They also noted that an enslaved man opened the gates of the plantations for them.[35] This information fortifies that when enslaved workers were authorized to go to the city—either to do services for the enslaver/overseers or to sell the products they cultivated—they used the same road connecting the plantations (Figure 77). Hence, it is likely that enslaved people knew and had relations with the enslaved from neighboring plantations. While passing through other plantations and spending time in the city, they built networks of relationships with other enslaved workers, free men, and merchants from the agrarian and urban world. In this way, enslaved people built their own geography from the knowledge of their movements, whether authorized or not, beyond the plantation spaces. The relationship with small farmers facilitated some escapes because the runaway enslaved used to work for them in exchange for help hiding or for a low wage. A relationship among the workers of neighboring plantations also existed, as sometimes the workers moved back and forth from one plantation to another. As described by Ms. Cecê, a resident of the Tabuleiro do Buraco, the workers from the Buraco Plantation worked on the Vitória

Plantation and vice versa, which shows that this was very common as the plantations belonged to the same owners.[36]

According to architect and historian Günter Weimer, the name and architecture of Brazilian senzalas were brought from Africa, where similar rows of rooms were called *sanzalas*.[37] The senzalas at the Vitória Plantation were similar to those mentioned by Weimer, which suggests that enslaved people could have built their dwellings. The site was, however, almost certainly designated by the plantations' owners, and the structures themselves, one must assume, acquired a new austerity under the logic of the Brazilian slavery economy.

A senzala on the Vitória Plantation resembles a Yoruba home[38] in its structure and layout.[39] The quarters' vernacular architecture was only one factor of the African culture that resisted slavery. The two other important forms of cultural resistance were religion and celebrations—music and dance. When Africans arrived in Brazil, the Catholic religion was directly imposed. Africans were baptized and received Portuguese names. It was a way to erase their past lives and cultures, to further subjugate them to a new land, culture, and religion. The planters forced the enslaved to gather for Catholic prayers every Sunday under the supervision of overseers, and they were subjected to punishment if they did not do so, for example, losing their free day on Sunday. To subvert this practice, the enslaved used the strategy of pretending they believed in the Catholic saints; however, they instead correlated each saint to African deities. Many times, the enslaved people made clay sculptures of their deities and hid them under the Catholic altars to pretend that they were praying to the saints. It is possible that the Vitória Plantation's enslaved people used a similar strategy there, as there is a small grotto on the hill adorned with clay saints.

The Brazilian African religion (Candomblé)[40] is always mixed with music and dance. According to historian Carlos Nascimento, many popular and religious parties were held on the Vitória Plantation, with the participation of many people from the neighborhood.[41] During these celebrations, which usually happened in the yard in front of the senzalas, enslaved people sang, danced, and beat drums to the deities without White people's knowledge. They were allowed to join the celebrations, and the enslavers and his family enjoyed watching them. The music and drumming were usually a clamor for homesickness or unhappiness with their lives under slavery. However, they only sang their laments in African languages, not comprehensible to White people.

This celebration, a syncretism between Candomblé and Catholicism, resisted slavery and is popular in Brazil today. After the abolition of slavery, Candomblé was prohibited; however, similar to many other obstacles Black people needed to endure, the religion resisted.[42] Today, most Brazilians are Catholic; however, Candomblé is strong in Bahia, mainly in the Cachoeira region. In addition, believers usually follow both religions and have faith in the divination[43] of saints and/or deities, as they are still related—each saint has its sister/brother deities and the same celebrity day.[44] This strong connection shows that religion was a way enslaved people found to resist White dominance and pass down their values through generations. Their link through religion was also a way to connect the different African beliefs and resist the annihilation of their cultures. Every year in August, in the city of Cachoeira, there is a celebration with the Sisterhood Our Lady of the Good Death (Irmandade da Boa Morte) and the Catholic church. It shows the syncretism of the two religions, so different but with a strong connection. This congregation reveals that the African religion heavily resisted cultural forces against it and was successfully transmitted through generations.

Chapter Conclusion

African cultures spread beyond the plantations and strongly influenced the songs and dances of the entire country. Brazil is well-known for the carnival, Salvador's being the most popular one. Thousands of people from everywhere join in the streets to celebrate. Most of the songs talk about African histories, and the dance styles are the same done to honor the deities. However, like in the past, many foreigners who attend this party annually do not know that they are celebrating the heritage of African culture in Brazil.

This chapter shows the disciplinary spatial organization built by the enslaver of the Vitória Plantation and the alternative geography built by enslaved workers to confront it. The slave resistance developed a new dimension that started not only from the assumptions of their autonomy but also from more concrete elements. An example of the conscious uses of plantation spaces are the networks of relationships developed by enslaved people beyond the plantation and their role in the production process. Different from what happened in the first two case studies, runaways from Vitória, instead of crossing the river, built settlements inside the plantation's land, and they probably continued to have close contact with enslaved people that remained there.

The architecture of the plantation was designed to promote control, order, production, optimization, and inspection, and to reduce the mobility of enslaved people; however, the space of the plantation both constituted an instrument of enslaver domination and enabled a strategy for slave resistance. The slaveholders used spatiality as a mechanism for imposing and facilitating order. Nonetheless, enslaved people used and saw the same spaces in different ways. On the one hand, the enslaver and overseers at the Vitória Plantation used most of the built spaces to control and oppress enslaved people. On the other hand, enslaved people used some agency—given to them or not—to maintain their culture in the construction of their quarters, their faith in their deities, and their personal crops, and in all possible ways they transformed and took advantage of time and space to challenge the system.

Vitória was built in the last century of slavery when there were many free Black people. In addition, the transmission of culture on the Vitória Plantation was stronger, as the enslaved people there were allowed to participate, play, and sing their traditional songs at the open parties observed by the enslavers. For enslaved people, doing an activity together, even with the permission of the enslavers, was a form of resistance. Group activities such as dance, music, and celebrations according to African traditions or even the cultivation of small crops or planning an escape, had special value. Therefore, enslaved people resignified the plantation's spaces and made alternative uses from those for which they were designed.

On May 13, 1888, Princess Isabel signed the Golden law (lei Aurea), which officially abolished slavery in Brazil; however, the legacies of the four centuries of slavery marked Brazilian society profoundly, and the vestiges are still present today, physically and psychologically. The epilogue will show how the structural architecture of the plantations still influences the contemporary architecture of the cities and Brazilian residences. The favelas growing everywhere in the cities, the maids' rooms still designed in the back of the residences, and the way Brazilians from different classes and ethnicities relate to each other show that the legacies of the plantation slavery system are still strong in Brazilian society.

Epilogue

> ... the African slave knew how to dance, sing, create new institutions
> and religious and secular relationships, deceive his master, sometimes
> poison him, defend his family, sabotage production, pretend to be sick,
> escape from the plantation, fight when possible, and accommodate
> when convenient. This true historical juggling resulted in the
> construction of a Black Diaspora culture characterized by optimism,
> courage, musicality, and incomparable aesthetic and political audacity
> in the context of the so-called Western Civilization.

—JOÃO JOSÉ REIS[1]

Introduction

The main objective of this book was to study the spaces of power
and resistance on the Bahian Recôncavo plantations. Although violence on plantations is a topic always present and well illustrated in
scholarship, for this study, the focus was on the role of built spaces
in the preservation of a system based on domination and surveillance of the enslaved people and how they also used the spaces to
resist exploitation. Further, this study sought to contribute to the
scholarship on how those plantations influenced both the built environment and a society built on them.

The analysis of the iconography, archival plans, written reports,
historiography, and the sites of the three plantations studied demonstrated that the organization of the built environment of the
plantations was the central element in the enslavers' strategies
for discipline and surveillance. In contrast, the uses of plantation
landscapes were one of the tools that enslaved people used to resist
and seek ways to react to the rigors of the imposed system. For this
reason, special attention was given to the documents that mentioned the use of the spatiality of the plantations for either enslavers
or enslaved people. The objective was to understand enslaved
people's resistance and the functioning of the enslaver's control
based on a geography marked by containment and surveillance

and characterized by alternative uses of plantation spaces to fight against it. Moreover, the research reveals that the geographic dimension was not only restricted to the spatiality of the plantations but also extended to the neighborhood areas linked to enslaved people's mobility and the construction of relationships outside the plantations.

Comparing the Plantations

The three plantations covered the whole period of slavery in Brazil (1536–1888). Although the plantations started their production of sugar in different centuries, they continued their activities throughout the nineteenth century, when the sugar commerce was still operating until the abolition of slavery. In the analysis of the buildings of these plantations, one could see that even in periods of sugar crises, the architecture of the plantations kept the same splendor. This might be because the three plantations belonged to three rich and powerful families of the Recôncavo who had many other plantations and different businesses.

SURVEILLANCE

In the analysis of the organization of the built environment, the plantations had different ways to surveil the workers using the geography of each plantation. The Cajaíba Plantation was the one with the most similar organization to the plantations from other places of the Americas, as its buildings were organized on a flat terrain with each building—Big House, sugar mill, senzalas, and overseer's house—on one side of a square. The Vitória Plantation used a panopticon strategy of vigilance with the overseer's house built higher than the other buildings and the Big House with many windows toward the senzalas, the sugar mill, and the cane fields. The Freguesia Plantation seemed to be the one with a less imposed strategy of surveillance, which might be because it was built in the sixteenth century. However, the position of the overseer's house near the senzalas and sugar mill, and a four-floor, imposing Big House built on an escarpment, show a similar approach to watching enslaved people.

Concerning physical punishments, it seems that Freguesia used the strategy of small punishment more than any kind of harder flogging. The plantation seems to only make use of instruments to contain mobility. Although there is a register of mutilations, it has no history of pillory whipping in the documents analyzed, which does not mean that overseers did not use it on the cane fields. The Cajaíba Plantation is the one with a well-known history of cruelty. The instruments of physical punishments, like a pillory and a well to drown enslaved people, can still be found there. In contrast, on the Vitória Plantation, there is no mention of physical punishments in the documents and historiography. Only small lashes or emotional torture might have been used there, to justify the murder of the overseers. Travelers' reports show that the enslaved at the Vitória Plantation might have been well treated, although with a melancholy countenance. The plantation may perhaps have used psychological vigilance more than physical punishments.

RESISTANCE

Resistance was practically a daily occurrence on the three plantations. Although they were under vigilance, in a similar way, the enslaved were also watching the enslaver's and overseer's habits. They often took advantage of a situation to plan against the system. Although small acts of resistance left no empirical evidence, stories and anecdotes indicate that they existed on all three plantations. They were the most common acts of resistance, most of the time never noticed by the enslavers. The study also found that enslaved people often circulated beyond the plantations. Because their enslavers owned other neighboring plantations and some of them received authorization to sell their crops in the city, the enslaved probably built a network of social relationships.

Enslaved people on all three plantations used spatial geography to hide and build quilombola settlements that have been perpetuated by their descendants to this day. The runaway enslaved of the Cajaíba and Freguesia plantations built permanent settlements far from the core of the plantations, across the rivers. This means that they probably escaped permanently. Differently, enslaved people from the Vitória Plantation, although they could cross the

Paraguaçu River to escape, preferred to build settlements inside the forest on top of the hill behind the plantation. This might indicate that they were still in contact with enslaved workers from the Vitória Plantation and from the neighboring areas, and they could do only a petit marronage, escaping only for a night or for a few days before returning to the plantation.

Enduring Legacy of Slave Plantations

The end of slavery did not guarantee the fundamental rights for the Black population, who continued to be segregated and marginalized. The former enslaved began to occupy the urban environment and dispute the use of the land. With the arrival of European immigrants to work in both rural and urban areas, Black workers were increasingly discriminated against and were pushed to live in remote areas or create communities within cities, in both cases without any kind of support from the government, such as basic sanitation structure. Due to the lack or delay in the arrival of these infrastructures and the wish to live close to job offers, many people continued living in the urban centers, building shacks on unoccupied lands. That is the origin of the favelas (informal settlements) in Brazil's large cities. For instance, Salvador, a city with the largest Black population outside Africa, has three million inhabitants with one million living in favelas, among whom 70 percent are Afro-descendants.[2] The favelas grow alongside luxurious buildings, separated by a wall, a park, a road, or any other element that isolates these communities from the middle- and upper-class territory. Consequently, Black people never stopped their struggle for survival, continually resisting a system that wanted to segregate them.

For the Black population, the dissemination of the slavery model developed in Brazil transformed into systemic racism that persists to the present day. We can find this in mass incarceration and the genocide of the Black population in poor communities. It can also be easily seen in the architecture of residences. Despite the modernity of the residences throughout the decades, the designs of Brazilian residences continue to follow the colonial pattern: the division of social, private, and service areas, with the bedroom for the maids in the back of the residences. Accessed by the service area, the maids' rooms make clear the social hierarchy between employers—mostly White—and employees—mostly Black. Oftentimes the rooms lack adequate ventilation and lighting that a space in prolonged use requires. Frequently called "deposit" in the floor plans, it is not rare for them to be smaller than the bathrooms of the high-standards projects. The small maids' rooms serve as a social reminder of our slavery system, where Black women continue to take on the role of their grandmothers for a meager wage, a place to sleep, and food. The favelas and maids' rooms are social reminders of slavery's stratification.

Final Considerations

The social trauma deliberately generated by a finely tuned landscape of slavery has not been resolved in Brazil. The tenacious but pain-filled presence of impoverished fishermen on some former plantations attests to this fact. Enslaved workers were able to create a sense of community and belonging despite the oppressive conditions of plantation life. It is important to recognize and acknowledge the agency and resilience of enslaved people, who were able to resist and subvert the control of their oppressors in various ways. However, the lack of support for the former enslaved resulted in today's lower class being mostly formed from Black people, even though part of the middle and upper classes continue to insist that the nation's disparities do not hinge on race. It is worth noting that the legacy of slavery continues to have an impact on contemporary society and that the experiences and histories of enslaved people continue to shape the world we live in today. Informal settlements have been growing everywhere and the residential architecture of the Brazilian middle and upper classes still uses a layout with segregated service spaces similar to those of the plantations with the location of the maids' rooms resembling the domestic enslaved people's quarters.

This investigation hopes to lay the foundations to understand how the Brazilian sugar plantations were responsible for the creation and preservation of a cruel system whose practices—visible and invisible—have been transmitted through generations, affecting people's behavior, and are still physically present in Brazilian architecture. It is important to recognize and acknowledge the experiences and histories of enslaved people, and to learn from them in order to create a more just and equitable society for all.

Notes

CHAPTER ONE: PACES OF POWER AND RESISTANCE

1. Castro Alves, *Slave Ship*, part V (1868).

2. Slave Voyages, www.slavevoyages.org.

3. As Bert Barickman clearly explained, "The word [Recôncavo] in Portuguese means simply back bay or the inland shore of a bay, any bay. But in Brazil, the word has become firmly attached to the region around one particular bay—the bay that early Portuguese explorers christened the Baía de Todos os Santos (Bay of All Saints)." Barickman, *Bahian Counterpoint*, 9.

4. For more on the agrarian issue, see Prado, *A Questão Agrária*.

5. Human-made environment including buildings, streets, transportation options, open spaces, and more.

6. Massapé, or massapê: Rich clay soil excellent for the cultivation of sugarcane.

7. Azevedo, *Engenhos do Recôncavo Baiano*, 23.

8. Ott, *O Povoamento Do Recôncavo Baiano Pelos Engenhos*.

9. For more on Santo Domingo's Revolution, see Gonzalez, *Maroon Nation*. For more on the colonial Brazil economy, see Prado, *História Econômica do Brasil*; Prado, *Colonial Background of Modern Brazil*.

10. Slave Voyages, www.slavevoyages.org.

11. Vasconcelos, "Os Agentes Modeladores Das Cidades Brasileiras."

12. Barickman, *Bahian Counterpoint*, 35 and 136.

13. Barickman, *Bahian Counterpoint*, 2.

14. Antonil, *Cultura e Opulência Do Brasil*; Hutchinson, *Village and Plantation Life in Northeastern Brazil*, 3.

15. Antonil, *Cultura e Opulência Do Brasil*; J Lapa, *A Bahia e a Carreira da India*, 100; Nardi, *O Fumo Brasileiro*, 359; Barickman, *Bahian Counterpoint*, 28–33.

16. Root native to South America.

17. Barickman, *Bahian Counterpoint*, see specifically peasant farming; Schwartz, *Slaves, Peasants, and Rebels*.

18. Smacks and launches are small boats used to more quickly bring cassava from one place to another. Barickman, *Bahian Counterpoint*, 75.

19. Barickman, *Bahian Counterpoint*, 75.

20. Mattoso, *Ser Escravo no Brasil*; Freyre, *The Masters and the Slaves*; Schwartz, *Sugar Plantations in the Formation of Brazilian Society*; Barickman, "Persistence and Decline."

21. Schwartz, *Slaves, Peasants, and Rebels*. For more on subsistence agriculture, see also Barickman, *Bahian Counterpoint*, 17–28, 44–65.

22. Delle, *Colonial Caribbean*; Singleton, "Slavery and Spatial Dialectics on Cuban Coffee Plantations"; Haase, "'Within the Circle'"; Wilkins, "Intersection of Space and Power"; Marquese, "Visuality and Slave Management."

23. This study focuses only on the large sugarcane plantations, the ones that had a sugar mill and more than a hundred enslaved workers.

24. See more on the commodification process in Smallwood, *Saltwater Slavery*.

25. Schwartz, *Sugar Plantations in the Formation of Brazilian Society*, 134.

26. Usually called "Hegel's master-slave dialectic." Aching, "The Slave's Work."

27. Wilkins, "Intersection of Space and Power."

28. Delle, *Colonial Caribbean*, 106.

29. Singleton, "Slavery and Spatial Dialectics on Cuban Coffee Plantations," 105.

30. Haase, "'Within the Circle.'"

31. Epperson, "Panoptic Plantations"; Delle, *Colonial Caribbean*, 100–106; Singleton, *Slavery behind the Wall*, 66; Randle, "Applying the Panopticon Model"; Delle, "Habitus of Jamaica Plantations," 126.

32. Epperson, "Panoptic Plantations," 59; Dobson and Fisher, "Panopticon's Changing Geography," 307; Delle, *Colonial Caribbean*, 100–106.

33. Panopticon is a type of institutional building designed by philosopher and social theorist Jeremy Bentham in the late eighteenth century. It is a circular structure with a central observation tower, from which the guards can observe all of the cells or rooms arranged around the perimeter. The idea behind the panopticon is to allow for constant surveillance of the inmates or prisoners, who are not able to tell when they are being watched. Bentham, *Works of Jeremy Bentham*; Foucault, *Discipline and Punish*, 195–228.

34. Foucault, *Microfísica do Poder*.

35. Schwartz, "Plantations and Peripheries," 81.

36. Ellis and Ginsburg, *Cabin, Quarter, Plantation*, 12.

37. To see some examples of the use of power and/or resistance in plantation slavery in the United States and the Caribbean, see Delle, *Colonial Caribbean*; Singleton, *Slavery behind the Wall*; Ellis and Ginsburg, *Cabin, Quarter, Plantation*; Kaye, *Joining Places*; Glymph, *Out of the House of Bondage*; Fraginals, *Sugar Mill*.

38. Singleton, *Slavery behind the Wall*; Fesler, "Excavating the Spaces and Interpreting the Places"; Upton, "White and Black Landscapes."

39. Schwartz, *Sugar Plantations in the Formation of Brazilian Society*, 404.

40. Fraga Filho, *Crossroads of Freedom*.

41. Reis, "Resistência Escrava na Bahia," 107.

42. Moura, *Rebeliões da Senzala.*

43. Foucault, *Microfísica do Poder*, 332.

44. Foucault, *Discipline and Punish*, 204.

45. Wilkins, "Intersection of Space and Power."

46. Foucault, *Microfísica Do Poder*, 105.

47. Delle, "Habitus of Jamaican Plantation Landscape," 129.

48. Foucault, *Discipline and Punish*, 135–69.

49. Bourdieu, *Logic of Practice.*

50. Bourdieu, *Logic of Practice*, chapter 3.

51. Delle, "Habitus of Jamaican Plantation Landscapes," 125.

52. Foucault, *Microfísica Do Poder*, 341.

53. Ewbank, *Life in Brazil*, 439.

54. Scott, *Domination, and the Arts of Resistance.*

55. Scott, *Domination, and the Arts of Resistance*, 24.

56. Scott, *Domination, and the Arts of Resistance.*

57. Schwartz, "Resistance and Accommodation," 77–81.

58. Mattoso, *Ser Escravo no Brasil*, 158–66.

59. Slenes, *Na Senzala uma Flôr*, 112.

60. Diouf, *Slavery's Exiles*, 132.

61. Reis, "Escravos Fugidos."

62. For more on Palmares, see Cheney, *Quilombo dos Palmares*; Carneiro, *O Quilombo dos Palmares*; Lara, "O Território dos Palmares."

63. Schwartz, *Slaves, Peasants, and Rebels*, 259.

64. Capitães-do-mato were very well-known and feared by enslaved people. They patrolled the roads and captured fugitives in exchange for a reward.

65. Schwartz, *Slaves, Peasants, and Rebels*, 109.

66. Schwartz, "Mocambo," 327.

67. Moura, *Os Quilombos na Dinâmica Social do Brasil*; Reis, "Quilombos e Revoltas Escravas no Brasil."

68. Schwartz, "Resistance and Accommodation in Eighteenth-Century Brazil," 77.

69. Reis, *Rebelião Escrava no Brasil.*

70. Slavedrivers, or just drivers, were enslaved people who received manumission or some privileges. They helped overseers surveil enslaved people.

71. Fitts, "Landscape of Northern Bondage," 66.

72. Singleton, *Slavery behind the Wall.*

73. Northup, *12 Years a Slave*, 185.

74. Camp, *Closer to Freedom*, 7. Camp coined the term "rival geography" from Edward Said, *Culture and Imperialism.*

75. Kaye, *Joining Places*, 44.

76. Kaye, *Joining Places*, 5.

77. Hall, *Africans in Colonial Louisiana*, 202.

78. Reis, "Quilombos e Revoltas Escravas no Brasil," 16.

79. Schwartz, *Sugar Plantations in the Formation of Brazilian Society*, 76.

80. There is no precise information about when the first enslaved Africans arrived in Brazil. According to Carlos Ott, 1536 is the date of the first plantations in the Recôncavo region. Ott, *Povoamento do Recôncavo pelos Engenhos*, 1.

CHAPTER TWO: FREGUESIA SUGARCANE PLANTATION

1. Antonil, *Cultura e Opulência do Brazil*, 31.

2. Sousa, *Tratado Descriptivo do Brasil*, 125-26.

3. Sometimes on the old maps it was also written as "Engenho Matoim" or "Engenho do Cabote (Caboto)." Pinho, *História de um Engenho do Recôncavo*, 120.

4. This action is part of the National Tourism Development Program (Prodetur Bahia).

5. The Brazil tree (*Paubrasilia echinata*), the tree that gave Brazil its name. In Portuguese, "pau" means wood and "brasil" means reddish/ember-like.

6. Gilmar de Oliveira, "Caboto - O maior Potencial Turístico de Candeias," https://www.candeiasbahia.net/2009/10/distrito-de-caboto.html (accessed April 20, 2023).

7. Prado, *História Econômica do Brasil*; Santos, *Recôncavo*; Simonsen, *História Econômica do Brasil*; Furtado, *Formação Econômica do Brasil*.

8. Sousa, *Tratado Descriptivo do Brasil em 1587*, 126.

9. Pinho, *História de um Engenho do Recôncavo*, 173-75.

10. Vauthier, "Casa de Residência no Brasil," 192.

11. Sousa, *Tratado Descriptivo*, 126.

12. Sousa, *Tratado Descriptivo*, 126.

13. Freyre, *Masters and the Slaves*, xxxii.

14. See an analysis of the probable date of the construction in Pinho, *História de um Engenho*, 411-14.

15. Pinho, *História de um Engenho*, 412.

16. It was very common in Brazil to have guest rooms without access to the main part of the house. Almost any traveler could arrive on the farms and ask to stay for rest and meals before continuing the trip. See Spix and Martius, *Viagem pelo Brasil*, 167. However, if the travelers were relatives, friends, or recommended by friends, they were welcomed to sleep inside the house, in the many bedrooms of the private area. It is a tradition incorporated to this day in Brazilian society; when traveling, close friends and relatives almost always stay in friends'/family's residences instead of hotels. See Candler and Burgess, *Narrative of a Recent Visit to Brazil*, 56; Cardim, *Tratado da Terra e Gente do Brasil*, 157.

17. Pinho, *História de um Engenho*, 416.

18. Pinho, *História de um Engenho*, 431.

19. Latticework was commonly used at that time in panels and windows to maintain women's privacy. These panels were a legacy of Islamic architecture in Portugal during the three centuries of the Moors' domination of the Iberian Peninsula. See Mello, *A Herança Mourisca da Arquitetura no Brasil*.

20. Soares, *Tratado Descritivo do Brasil*, 126.

21. Inventory 1832. Pinho, *História de um Engenho*, 135.

22. See more about the vernacular architecture of the senzalas in chapter 4.

23. Vauthier, "Casa de Residência no Brasil," 204–5. Quote translated by the author.

24. Antonil, *Cultura e Opulência do Brazil*, 21.

25. Pinho, *História de um Engenho*, 253.

26. Scott, *Domination and the Arts of Resistance*, 24.

27. Sweet, *Recreating Africa*, 167.

28. Orser and Funari, "Arqueologia da Resistência Escrava."

29. Scott, *Domination and the Arts of Resistance*, 3, 199.

30. Pinho, *História de um Engenho*, 206.

31. Pinho, *História de um Engenho*, 267.

32. Pinho, *Histórias de um Engenho*, 431.

33. Pinho, *História de um Engenho*, 359, 254.

34. See more on "brecha camponesa" in Cardoso, *Escravo ou camponês?*

35. Antonil, *Cultura e Opulência*, 34.

36. Reis and Silva, *Negociação e conflito*, 29.

37. Survey of the sugar plantations in the parish of Matoim, 1854, APEB.

38. Schwartz, "Resistance and Accommodation in Eighteenth-Century Brazil," 77–79.

39. Interview with current Wanderley Pinho Museum employees Mr. Jorge Lima, Mr. Fred Bonfim, and Mr. José Milton during my visit to the site. They are descendants of former enslaved people and still have families living in Maré Island's communities.

40. Castellucci, "Entre Veredas e Arrabaldes," 274.

41. Information given by the employees of the museum Mr. Lima, Mr. Bonfim, and Mr. Milton.

CHAPTER THREE: CAJAÍBA SUGARCANE PLANTATION

1. Dubois, "Home of the Slave," 18.

2. Process No. 009/95; 010/95.

3. The village became a city on March 30, 1938.

4. Azevedo, *Arquitetura do Açucar*, 28.

5. The pact caused great loss to the colonies as the metropolis used to buy products at the prices they wanted. In addition, the development of the colonies stalled as they had to buy the raw material from the metropolis, which kept the colonies agrarian for a long time.

6. Simonsen, *História Econômica do Brasil*; Furtado, *Formação Econômica do Brasil*; Azevedo, *Arquitetura do Açucar*.

7. Mattoso, *Ser Escravo no Brasil*, 57.

8. Azevedo, *Arquitetura do Açucar*, 192n.174.

9. Antonil, *Cultura e Opulência*, 122.

10. For a study about these other plantations, see Tomich, Marquese, Monzote, and Fornias. *Reconstructing the Landscapes of Slavery*.

11. Santana and Farias, "Trabalho e Revolta."

12. Cardim, *Tratados da Terra e Gente do Brasil*, 283.

13. The owner of the boat who took me to the island showed me the possible location of the enslaved people's quarters; he said that learned this from older people.

14. Public Archive of the State of Bahia, Judiciário, 01/96/139/02 – 1870.

15. Public Archive of the State of Bahia, pack 5844, 22v.

16. Rio de Janeiro National Archive – GIFI-SJ-5H-198. APEB (Public Archive of the State of Bahia), maço 3139-57, 1879. The murder happened during a visit to his other plantation, Itatingui.

17. Fernandes, "Ilha de Cajaíba," 197.

18. The family had two other plantations: Vanique and Gurgainha. Besides sugarcane, they also had corn and cassava farms.

19. To read more about the quilombola communities around Cajaíba Island, see Fernandes, "Ilha de Cajaíba."

20. Azevedo, *Arquitetura do Açucar*, 138.

21. Sousa, *Tratado Descriptivo do Brasil*, 130.

22. Azevedo, *Arquitetura do Açucar*, 11–16.

23. Fraga Filho, *Crossroads of Freedom*, 16.

24. Reis, "Quilombos e Revoltas Escravas no Brasil," 20.

CHAPTER FOUR: VITÓRIA SUGARCANE PLANTATION

1. Douglass, *Narrative of the Life of Frederick Douglass*, 26.

2. Candler and Burgess, *Narrative of a Recent Visit to Brazil*, 56.

3. The former Big House and the chapel of the Adorno Plantation are still well maintained in the center of the city of Cachoeira. The city prison is currently located in the Big House.

4. Património de Influência Portuguesa, HPIP, http://www.hpip.org/def /en/Contents/Navigation/GeographicToponymicNavigation/Place?a=12 (accessed April 20, 2023).

5. Tomich called the modern African slavery linked to the industrial revolution the second slavery, following the first slavery that was directly linked to the colonization of the Americas. In the second slavery, sugar, coffee, and cotton commanded the slavery chain, intensifying the articulation of enslaved labor in the nineteenth century. With the industrial revolution, sugar and coffee changed from luxury items to basic products consumed by all social classes. Tomich, "'Second Slavery.'"

6. Pedro Bandeira was the son of Pedro Rodrigues Bandeira, who immigrated from Portugal to Brazil in the beginning of the eighteenth century. Pedro Bandeira (son) had many ships, which he used for commerce among Europe, Brazil, and Asia.

7. Bandeira also had a small plantation called Moinho; it is believed that he annexed it to Vitória after he bought its lands, as the name Moinho is not shown in the documents after he bought Vitória and constructed its buildings.

8. Pedro Rodrigues Bandeira inventory, maço 146, doc. N. 3 (APEB – State of Bahia Public Archive).

9. Interview with historian Carlos Nascimento, who is also a native of Cachoeira, July 2018.

10. Interview with Nascimento.

11. Because the Vitória Plantation was in the hands of Bandeira's descendants for more time than Bandeira himself, from here I will refer to the property of the plantation as belonging to his family.

12. Barickman, *Bahian Counterpoint*, 117.

13. Avé-Lallemant, *Viagem pelo Norte do Brasil no ano de 1859*, 61.

14. "SPHAN próMemória," *Journal of SPHAN* (history and artistic national heritage) 25 (July/August 1983): 2.

15. Faria, "Tramas e Laços entre os Quilombos das Cabeceiras do Iguape," 57.

16. Document 284-T-41. Programa Monumenta, "Sítios Históricos," 223.

17. Azevedo, *Arquitetura do Açucar*, 109–18.

18. As already explained, it was very common in Brazil to have outside bedrooms and provide meals to travelers passing by the plantations, such as merchants.

19. Candler and Burgess, *Narrative of a Recent Visit to Brazil*, 57.

20. Gama, *Engenho e Tecnologia*, 252.

21. Some authors count the senzalas per building, other count them separated per rooms. I opted for the second option.

22. Faria, "Tramas e Laços," 78.

23. Avé-Lallemant, *Viagem pelo Norte do Brasil*, 43.

24. Candler and Burgess, *Narrative of a Recent Visit to Brazil*, 56–57.

25. Delle, *Colonial Caribbean*, 101.

26. DuBois, "Home of the Slave," 21.

27. Cachoeira, March 24, 1827, APEB, Câmara de Cachoeira, maço 1269.

28. Smith and David, "Production of Space." They got the term "appropriation" from Harvey and Lefebvre. Harvey, *Condition of Postmodernity*; Lefebvre, *Production of Space*.

29. Upton, "White and Black Landscapes."

30. Reis, "Recôncavo Rebelde," 114–15.

31. Reis, "Quilombos e Revoltas Escravas no Brasil," 18–19.

32. Quilombola communities formed by descendants of slaves of Vitoria Plantation certified by the FCP (Palmares Cultural Foundation): Engenho Da Vitória Community, process n. 01420.000361/2004-18 (06/21/2004) and Tabuleiro da Vitória, process 01420.009700/2013-12 (08/13/2013) – www .palmares.gov.br.

33. Faria, "Tramas e Laços entre os Quilombos das Cabeceiras do Iguape," 23.

34. Barickman, *Bahian Counterpoint*, 58–60; Candler and Burgess, *Narrative of a Recent Visit to Brazil*, 57; Fraga Filho, *Crossroads of Freedom*, 15–22.

35. Candler and Burgess, *Narrative of a Recent Visit to Brazil*, 61.

36. Faria, "Tramas e Laços," 24.

37. Weimer, *Arquitetura Popular Brasileira*, 11.

38. Nigerian vernacular architecture.

39. Azevedo, *Engenhos do Recôncavo Baiano*, 129.

40. Candomblé is an African diasporic religion that developed in Brazil during the nineteenth century. It arose through a process of syncretism between the traditional Yoruba religions of West Africa, Roman Catholicism, and Spiritism. See Bastide, *African Religions of Brazil*.

41. Interview with Nascimento. He explained that they were passed by former enslaved workers to their descendants.

42. The country does not have an official religion; in 1946, freedom of religious worship was decreed. All religious expression must be respected. However, Candomblé is still disrespected by some other religions, the so-called *evangélicos*.

43. Nascimento, *Bitedô*.

44. Part of Candomblé is separating the link between saints and deities.

EPILOGUE

1. Reis, "Resistência Escrava na Bahia," 107.

2. IBGE, 2019.

Bibliography

Aching, Gerard. "The Slave's Work: Reading Slavery through Hegel's Master-Slave Dialectic." *PMLA* 127, no. 4 (2012): 912–17.

Antonil, André João (João Antônio Andreoni). *Cultura e Opulência Do Brasil por suas Drogas e Minas*. Lisboa: Oficina Real Deslandesiana, 1711.

Avé-Lallemant, Robert. *Viagem pelo Norte do Brasil no ano de 1859*. Vol. 1. Rio de Janeiro: Instituto Nacional do Livro, 1961.

Azevedo, Esterzilda Berenstein de. *Arquitetura do Açúcar: Engenhos do Recôncavo Baiano no Período Colonial*. São Paulo: Nobel, 1990.

———. *Engenhos do Recôncavo Baiano (Sugarcane Farms of Bahia's Recôncavo)*. Brasília, DF: IPHAN/Programa Monumenta, 2009.

Barickman, Bert J. *A Bahian Counterpoint: Sugar, Tobacco, Cassava, and Slavery in the Recôncavo, 1780–1860*. Stanford, Calif.: Stanford University Press, 1998.

———. "Persistence and Decline: Slave Labor and Sugar Production in the Bahian Recôncavo, 1850–1888." *Brazil: History and Society* 28, no. 3 (October 1996): 581–633.

———. "Revisiting the Casa-Grande: Plantation and Cane-Farming Households in Early Nineteenth-Century Bahia." *Hispanic American Historical Review* 84, no. 4 (2004): 619–59.

Bastide, Roger. *The African Religions of Brazil: Toward a Sociology of the Interpenetration of Civilizations*. Baltimore: Johns Hopkins University Press, 2007.

Bentham, Jeremy. *The Works of Jeremy Bentham*. Edinburgh: W. Tait, 1843.

Bourdieu, Pierre. *The Logic of Practice*. Translated by Richard Nice. Stanford, Calif.: Stanford University Press, 2014.

Camp, Stephanie M. H. *Closer to Freedom: Enslaved Women and Everyday Resistance in the Plantation South*. Chapel Hill: University of North Carolina Press, 2004.

Campos, João da Silva. *Tempo Antigo, Crônicas d'Antanho, Marcos do Passado, Histórias do Recôncavo*. Bahia: Secretaria de Educação e Saúde, 1942.

Candler, John, and Wilson Burgess. *Narrative of a Recent Visit to Brazil*. London: Edward Marh, Friends' Book and Tract Depository, 1853.

Cardim, Fernão. *Tratado da Terra e Gente do Brasil*. São Paulo: Ed. University of São Paulo, 1980.

Cardoso, Ciro Flamarion. *Escravo ou camponês? O Protocampesinato negro nas Américas*. São Paulo: Brasiliense, 1987.

Carneiro, Edson. *O Quilombo dos Palmares*. São Paulo: WMF Martins Fontes, 2011.

Castellucci Jr., Wellington. "Entre Veredas e Arrabaldes: Histórias de Escravose Forros na Comarca de Nazaré, Bahia, 1830-1850." *História & Perspectivas* 1, no. 39 (2008).

Cheney, Glenn Alan. *Quilombo dos Palmares: Brazil's Lost Nation of Fugitive Slaves*. Hanover, Conn.: New London Librarium, 2014.

Delle, James A. *An Archaeology of Social Space: Analyzing Coffee Plantations in Jamaica's Blue Mountains*. New York: Plenum Press, 1998.

————. *The Colonial Caribbean: Landscapes of Power in the Plantation System*. New York: Cambridge University Press, 2014.

————. "The Habitus of Jamaican Plantation Landscape. In *Out of Many, One People*, edited by Mark W. Hauser, and Douglas V. Armstrong, 122-43. Tuscaloosa: University of Alabama Press, 2011.

Diouf, Sylviana A. *Slavery's Exiles: The Story of the American Maroons*. New York: New York University Press, 2014.

Dobson, Jerome E., and Peter F. Fisher. "The Panopticon's Changing Geography." *Geographical Review* 97, no. 3 (July 2007): 307-23.

Douglass, Frederick. *My Bondage and My Freedom*. Scotts Valley, Calif.: CreateSpace, 2017.

————. *Narrative of the Life of Frederick Douglass: An American Slave*. Digireads.com Publishing, 2016.

DuBois, W. E. B. "The Home of the Slave." In *Cabin, Quarter, Plantation: Architecture and Landscape of North American Slavery*, edited by Clifton Ellis and Rebecca Ginsburg. New Haven, Conn.: Yale University Press, 2010.

Ellis, Clifton, and Rebecca Ginsburg, eds. *Cabin, Quarter, Plantation: Architecture and Landscapes of North American Slavery*. New Haven, Conn.: Yale University Press, 2010.

Epperson, Terrence W. "Panoptic Plantations: The Garden Sights of Thomas Jefferson and George Mason." In *Lines that Divide: Historical Archaeologies or Race, Class, and Gender*, edited by James A. Delle, Stephen A. Mrozowsli, and Robert Paynter, 58-77. Knoxville: University of Tennessee Press, 2000.

Ewbank, Thomas. *Life in Brazil*. New York: Harper, 1856.

Faria, Ana Tereza D. P. "Tramas e Laços entre os Quilombos das Cabeceiras do Iguape: Configurações de um Território." Master's thesis, Federal University of Bahia, 2019.

Ferlini, Vera Lúcia Amaral. *Terra, Trabalho e Poder: O Mundo dos Engenhos no Nordeste Colonial*. São Paulo: Ed. Brasiliense, 1988.

Fernandes, Mariana B. "Ilha de Cajaíba: Lugar, Pertencimento e Territorialidade nas Comunidades Quilombolas Acupe, SãoBraz e Dom João/Recôncavo Baiano." PhD diss. Federal University of Bahia, 2016.

Fesler, Garret. "Excavating the Spaces and Interpreting the Places of Enslaved Africans and Their Descendants." In *Cabin, Quarter, Plantation: Architecture and Landscapes of North American Slavery*, edited by Clifton Ellis and Rebecca Ginsburg, 27-49. New Haven, Conn.: Yale University Press, 2010.

Fitts, Robert K. "The Landscape of Northern Bondage." *Historical Archaeology* 30, no. 2 (1996): 54-73.

Foucault, Michel. *The Archaeology of Knowledge and the Discourse on Language*. Translated by A. M. Sheridan Smith. New York: Pantheon Books, 1972.

———. *Discipline and Punish: The Birth of the Prison*. New York: Vintage Books, 1995.

———. *Microfísica Do Poder*. Rio de Janeiro: Paz & Terra, 2018.

Fraga Filho, Walter. *Crossroads of Freedom*. Translated by Mary Ann Mahony. Durham, NC: Duke University Press, 2016.

Fraginals, Manuel Moreno. *The Sugar Mill: The Socioeconomic Complex of Sugar in Cuba, 1760-1860*. New York: Monthly Review Press, 1976.

Freyre, Gilberto. *The Masters and the Slaves: A Study in the Development of Brazilian Civilization*. Berkeley: University of California Press, 1986.

Furtado, Celso. *Formação Econômica do Brasil*. São Paulo: Companhia Editora Nacional, 2005.

Gama, Ruy. *Engenho e Tecnologia*. São Paulo: Duas Cidades, 1983.

Ginsburg, Rebecca. "Escaping through a Black Landscape." In *Cabin, Quarter, Plantation: Architecture and Landscape of North American Slavery*, edited by Clifton Ellis and Rebecca Ginsburg, 51-66. New Haven, Conn.: Yale University Press, 2010.

Glymph, Thavolia. *Out of the House of Bondage: The Transformation of the Plantation Household*. New York: Cambridge University Press, 2008.

Gomes, Geraldo. *Antigos Engenhos de Açúcar no Brasil*. Rio de Janeiro: Editora Nova Fronteira, 1994.

Gonzalez, John Henry. *Maroon Nation: A History of Revolutionary Haiti*. New Haven, Conn.: Yale University Press, 2018.

Haase, Felix. "'Within the Circle': Space and Surveillance in Frederick Douglass's *Narrative of the Life of Frederick Douglass*, an American Slave." *Aspeers* 8 (2015): 72-88.

Hall, Gwendolyn Midlo. *Africans in Colonial Louisiana: The Development of Afro-Creole Culture in the Eighteenth Century*. Baton Rouge: Louisiana State University Press, 1992.

————. *Africans in Colonial Louisiana: The Development of Afro-Creole Culture in the Eighteenth Century*. 2nd ed. Baton Rouge: Louisiana State University Press, 1995.

Harvey, David. *The Condition of Postmodernity*. Oxford: Basil Blackwell, 1989.

Hutchinson, Harry William. *Village and Plantation Life in Northeastern Brazil*. Seattle: University of Washington Press, 1957.

Kaye, Anthony E. *Joining Places: Slave Neighborhoods in the Old South*. Chapel Hill: University of North Carolina Press, 2007.

Lapa, José Roberto do Amaral. *A Bahia e a Carreira da India*. São Paulo: Editora Da Unicamp, 2000.

Lara, Silvia H. "O Território dos Palmares: Cartografia, História e Política." *Afro-Ásia*, no. 64 (2021): 12–50.

Lefebvre, Henri. *The Production of Space*. Oxford: Basil Blackwell, 1991.

Marquese, Rafael. "A Dinâmica da Escravidão no Brasil: Resistência, trafico negreiro e alforrias, séculos XVII a XIX." *Novos Estudos* 74 (March 2006): 107–23.

————. "Visuality and Slave Management in the Brazilian and Cuban Coffee and Sugar Plantations, c. 1840–1880." Paper presented at *Ever Closer to Freedom: The Work and Legacies of Stephanie M. H. Camp Conference*, University of Washington, Seattle, May 7–8, 2015.

Mattoso, Kátia de Queirós. *Ser Escravo no Brasil*. São Paulo: Brasiliense, 2003.

Mello, Eduardo Kneese de. *A Herança Mourisca da Arquitetura no Brasil*. São Paulo: Universidade de São Paulo, 1973.

Moura, Clóvis. *Os Quilombos na Dinâmica Social do Brasil*. Maceió: EDUFAL, 2001.

————. *Rebeliões da Senzala: Quilombos, Insurreições, Guerrilhas*. São Paulo: LECH Editora, 1981.

Nardi, Jean Baptiste. *O Fumo Brasileiro No Período Colonial*. São Paulo: Brasiliense, 1996.

Nascimento, Beatriz. "O Conceito de Quilombo e a Resistência Cultural Negra." *AfroDiáspora* 3, no. 6/7 (1985): 41–49.

Nascimento, Luis Cláudio. *Bitedô: Onde Moram os Nagôs*. Rio de Janeiro: CEAP, 2010.

Northup, Solomon. *12 Years a Slave*. Los Angeles: Graymalkin, 2014.

Orser Jr., Charles, and Pedro Paulo Funari. "Arqueologia da Resistência Escrava." *Cadernos do LEPAARQ* 1, no. 2 (2004): 11–25.

Ott, Carlos. *O Povoamento do Recôncavo pelos Engenhos 1536-1888*. Vol. 1. Salvador: Bigraf, 1996.

Patterson, Orlando. *Slavery and Social Death: A Comparative Study.* Cambridge, Mass.: Harvard University Press, 1982.

Pedrão, Fernando C. "Novos Rumos, Novos Personagens." In *Recôncavo Da Bahia: Sociedade e Economia Em Transição,* edited by Maria de Azevedo Brandão, 217–39. Salvador: Academia de Letras da Bahia/Universidade Federal da Bahia, 1997.

Pinho, Wanderley. *História de um Engenho do Recôncavo: Matoim, Novo Caboto, Freguesia—1552-1944.* São Paulo: Companhia Editora Nacional, 1982.

Pires, Fernando T. F. "Engenhos de Açúcar no Recôncavo Baiano." *IHGB* 442 (2009): 233–48.

Prado Jr., Caio. *The Colonial Background of Modern Brazil.* Berkeley: University of California Press, 1967.

———. *História Econômica do Brasil.* São Paulo: Brasiliense, 1969.

———. *A Questão Agrária.* São Paulo: Brasiliense, 1979.

Programa Monumenta. *Sítios Históricos e Conjuntos Urbanos de Monumentos Nacionais: Norte, Nordeste e Centro-oeste.* Brasília: Ministério da Cultura, 2005.

Rago, Margareth. "O Efeito-Foucault na Historiografia Brasileira." *Revista Sociologia USP* (October 1995): 67–82.

Randle, Lisa B. "Applying the Panopticon Model to Historic Plantation Landscape through Viewshed Analysis." *Historical Geography* 39 (2011): 105–27.

Reis, João José. "Escravos Fugidos Asssombravam a Colônia e Inspiraram Lendas que a História não confirma." *Ameaça Negra* (June 14, 2008).

———. "Quilombos e Revoltas Escravas no Brasil." *Revista USP* 28, no. 95/96 (1996): 14–39.

———. *Rebelião Escrava no Brasil: A História do Levante dos Malês 1835.* São Paulo: Brasiliense, 1986.

———. "Recôncavo Rebelde." *AfroAsia* 15 (1990): 113.

———. "Resistência Escrava na Bahia." *AfroAsia* 14 (1983): 107–23.

Reis, João José, and Eduardo Silva. *Negociação e Conflito: A Resistência Negra no Brasil Escravista.* São Paulo: Companhia das Letras, 1999.

Reis, João José, and Flávio dos Santos Gomes. *Liberdade por um Fio: História dos Quilombos no Brasil.* São Paulo: Companhia das Letras, 1996.

Said, Edward. *Culture and Imperialism.* New York: Knopf, 1993.

Santana, Elciene, and Juliana Farias. "Trabalho e Revolta: Escravos Insurgentes em um Engenho do Recôncavo Baiano (São Francisco do Conde, 1870-80)." 30º Simpósio Nacional de História, Recife, 2019.

Santos, Marco Aurélio dos. *Geografia da Escravidão: No Vale do Paraíba Cafeeiro, Bananal, 1850-1888*. São Paulo: Alameda, 2016.

Santos, Milton. *Espaço e Método*. São Paulo: Nobel, 1985.

———. *A Natureza do Espaço: Técnica e Tempo. Razão e Emoção*. São Paulo: Editora da Universidade de São Paulo, 2006.

———. *Pensando o Espaço do Homem*. São Paulo: Editora da Universidade de São Paulo, 2007.

———. *Recôncavo: Berço dos Canaviais*. Salvador: Ed. Itapuã, 1975.

Schwartz, Stuart B. "Cantos e Quilombos numa Conspiração de Escravos Haussás—Bahia 1814." In *Liberdade por um Fio: História dos Quilombos no Brasil*, organized by João José Reis and Flávio dos Santos Gomes. São Paulo: Cia das Letras, 1996.

———. "The Mocambo: Slave Resistance in Colonial Bahia." *Journal of Social History* 3, no. 4 (1970): 313-33.

———. "Plantations and Peripheries." In *Colonial Brazil*, edited by Leslie Bethel, 67-144. Cambridge, UK, and New York: Cambridge University Press, 1987.

———. "Resistance and Accommodation in Eighteenth-Century Brazil: The Slave's View of Slavery." *Hispanic American Historical Review* 57, no. 1 (1977): 69-81.

———. *Sugar Plantations in the Formation of Brazilian Society: Bahia, 1550-1835*. Cambridge, UK: Cambridge University Press, 1985.

———. *Slaves, Peasants, and Rebels: Reconsidering Brazilian Slavery*. Urbana: University of Illinois Press, 1992.

Scott, James C. *Domination and the Arts of Resistance: Hidden Transcripts*. New Haven, Conn.: Yale University Press, 1990.

Simonsen, Roberto. *História Econômica do Brasil: 1500-1820*. Brasília: Senado Federal, 2005.

Singleton, Theresa A. "Slavery and Spatial Dialectics on Cuban Coffee Plantations." *World Archaeology* 33, no. 1 (2001): 98-114.

———. *Slavery behind the Wall: An Archaeology of a Cuban Coffee Plantation*. Gainesville: University Press of Florida, 2015.

Slenes, Robert W. *Na senzala, uma Flôr: Esperanças e Recordações na Formação da Familia Escrava. Brasil Sudeste, século XIX*. Rio de Janeiro: Nova Fronteira, 1999.

Smallwood, Stephanie E. *Saltwater Slavery: A Middle Passage from Africa to American Diaspora*. Cambridge, Mass.: Harvard University Press, 2009.

Smith, Adam, and Nicholas David. "The Production of Space and the House of Xidi Sukur." *Current Anthropology* 36, no. 3 (June 1995).

Sousa, Gabriel Soares. *Tratado Descriptivo do Brasil em 1587*. Rio de Janeiro: Typographia de João Ignacio da Silva, 1879.

Spix and Martius. *Viagem pelo Brasil (1817–1820)*. Vol. 2. Translated by Lúcia F. Lahmeyer. Brasília: Senado Federal, 2017.

Sweet, James Hoke. *Recreating Africa: Culture, Kinship, and Religion in the African Portuguese World, 1441–1770*. Chapel Hill: University of North Carolina Press, 2003.

Tomich, Dale. "The 'Second Slavery': Bonded Labor and the Transformation of the Nineteenth-Century World Economy." In *Rethinking the Nineteenth Century: Contradictions and Movements*, edited by Francisco O. Ramirez, 103–17. New York: Greenwood Press: 1988.

Tomich, Dale W., Rafael de Bivar Marquese, Reinaldo Funes Monzote, and Carlos Venegas Fornias. *Reconstructing the Landscapes of Slavery: A Visual History of the Plantation in the Nineteenth-Century Atlantic World*. Chapel Hill: University of North Carolina Press, 2021.

Upton, Dell. "White and Black Landscapes in Eighteenth-Century Virginia." In *Cabin, Quarter, Plantation: Architecture and Landscape of North American Slavery*, edited by Ellis Clifton and Rebecca Ginsburg, 121–40. New Haven, Conn.: Yale University Press, 2010.

Vasconcelos, Pedro de Almeida. "Os Agentes Modeladores Das Cidades Brasileiras No Período Colonial." In *Explorações Geográficas: Percurso no fim do século*, organized by Iná Castro, Paulo Gomes, and Roberto Corrêa, 247–78. Rio de Janeiro: Bertrand Brasil, 1997.

Vauthier, Louis-Léger. "Casa de Residência no Brasil." *Revista do Serviço do Patrimônio Histórico e Artístico Nacional* 7 (1943): 128–209.

Vilhena, Luis dos Santos. *Reconpilação de Noticias Soteropolitans e Brasilicas*. Bahia: Imprensa Oficial do Estado, 1921.

Vlach, John Michael. *Back of the Big House: The Architecture of Plantation Slavery*. Chapel Hill: University of North Carolina Press, 1993.

Weimer, Günter. *Arquitetura Popular Brasileira*. São Paulo, Martins Fontes, 2005.

Wilkins, Andrew. "The Intersection of Space and Power: Plantation Overseers in the American South." Paper presented at the *47th Annual Conference on Historical and Underwater Archaeology*, Quebec City, Canada, January 8–12, 2014.